FRIEDI KÜHNE

ABOVE THE ABYSS

Finding Strength, Stillness, and Survival on the Slackline

NOTE: To provide an authentic insight into his experiences and the slackline sport, Friedi uses various terms that may not be immediately familiar to every reader. See page 230 for a glossary of relevant terms.

First printed in 2023 in Germany as *Über dem Abgrund* by Conbook Medien GmbH, Neuss

Published in 2026 by

an imprint of The Stable Book Group
32 Court Street, Suite 2109
Brooklyn, NY 11201
www.velopress.com

ISBN: 978-1-64604-860-1
eISBN: 978-1-64604-861-8
Library of Congress Control Number: 2025944352

Cover design: Abbey Gregory
Artwork: graphic chapter openings (pp. 36–37, pp. 126–127, pp. 198–199) based on an illustration © Vaclav P3k / Shutterstock
Interior design and production: Westchester Publishing Services

Printed in the United States
10 9 8 7 6 5 4 3 2 1

"I've spent the last two decades of my life pursuing the artistic expression of slacklining, and to know a book was written by one of my slacklife idols based upon his experiences of risk, reward, community, travel, and art makes this book a must-read.

The lessons learned and shared within these pages will undoubtedly be as unforgettable as the history these adventures have written in stone."

(Andy Lewis, US slacklining icon)

Contents

Foreword

"He who fears death will never do anything worthy of a man who is alive."

—Unknown
(based on the words and ideas of Seneca)

So, what would you die for?

As my hobby mutated into sport, the evolution of movement became artistic expression and imagery, and as the art transmuted to obsession, my obsession became worth more than life itself. It was at that moment that slacklining transcended into a lifestyle—my lifestyle. I liked to call it slacklife. My journey started with Dean Potter (a famous extreme sports artist); Dan Osman (famous for blasphemous creativity in extreme sports); Scott and Rick Balcom, Maria Faye (all OG slackline community, Slackline bros, Slackdaddy, etc.); Damian Cooksey (original front flip and longline record); Jerry Miszewski (loose line innovator, now founder and CEO of balancecommunity.com); Ivo Ninov (member of the Stone Monkeys); Timmy O'Neill (high-energy ambassador); and Ammon McNeely ("El Cap Pirate"). I idolized the Yosemite Stone Monkeys and dreamed of being as capable and fearless as the world's leading extreme sports icons.

Everything I did can be attributed to their original invigoration of my soul. What I developed in kind would add one more step to the journey, something that the next person would start with—a standard waypoint to help define what would be possible in the future of slackline. I wrote songs about slacklife, and I practiced what I preached, bringing balance everywhere with a line I carried in my pocket for years. Slackline club became the most popular club at my college, inspiring clubs worldwide. I got a slacklife tattoo on my forearm. My slacklife journey created a path for others to follow globally, and communities began to grow internationally. The energy I put into the world in turn sent me around the world and even helped put me front and center at the Super Bowl halftime show doing a duet with Madonna in 2012.

The journey unfolded day by day—from seeing Dean free solo the spire highline at fifty-five feet / seventeen meters long and two thousand feet / six-hundred-ten meters high, to the purchase of a single piece of one-inch tubular nylon webbing—ending now with a sport that features a lifestyle so diverse it will never stop growing. That simple image of conquering fear and purchasing an arbitrary piece of webbing developed into such a brilliant momentum that I could only call it destiny. I felt so inspired I chose this sport that I would willingly sacrifice anything and everything in my life to develop a path through uncharted territory to honor the gift that slacklining was able to give me—a love of living life. This is a gift I believed the entire world would appreciate having the opportunity of adopting—living step by step, and when you fall, you get back up with patience, poise, perseverance, and purpose. Slacklife became my metaphor. Giving up my life to slacklife would only manifest if I could earn my place in its written history. I wanted to allow myself to risk life and limb because I wanted to know what my life was worth to me. What did it mean to me? Every day something is being discovered, mapped, named, or created, and as the island of my knowledge grew, so did the shores of my ignorance. All I wanted was to leave a mark on the sport that no one could deny or ignore—not even Dean.

In the end, everything I helped build can be attributed to one thing—believing it could be built in the first place. Anything possible in life was possible on the line—that was the belief, that was the thought, and that's where I put my faith. Luck is said to be the intersection of opportunity and preparation, and that you never rise to the occasion—you only fall to your level of preparation. I didn't want my ghost to come back saying that my training failed me. So I trained—a lot. If people knew the amount of work I put into my life, they wouldn't call anything I have done genius, but rather inevitable. I encouraged growth and development simply by demanding it. Challenging myself to rig lines in new ways, setting new restrictions, and then betting my life on many experimental occasions. Challenging myself to do a highline a week, then a free solo a week, to eventually one hundred highlines in a year. Ridiculous goals inspire ridiculous effort. Some days on the trickline, while trying to create new movements, I would disallow myself from doing anything I had previously done on the line up to that day. If I wanted to get on the line, I would have to get on it in a new way, think of some new movement or pose, and rise to the challenge. I found that watching recorded videos helped dissect the mistakes I was making and gave insights into how to make things that were impossible become possible. These videos became a part of how I shared my art with the world, for free, and for one reason—to help the sport evolve. I would need help to get other people to start the journey. The more I gave away, the more opportunities came back.

When Robert and Jaan Kaeding came into my life with Gibbon Slacklines and the slogan "Slackline for everyone," they gifted me the ability to commit my energy in ways that were not possible before. The team we created became the foundation for the development of the slacklife community, whose aims were evolving slacklining and living the slacklife. My drive for creation, research, and development mixed with Gibbon's capabilities for global community, innovation, logistics, and execution created the most powerful conglomeration slacklife had ever seen. I could have never imagined how much impact would be created by bringing the best minds and talents together annually, but every year that Gibbon helped round up the talent, I was blown away by the evolution of the sport compounded by the extraordinary development and size of the community. Slacklife was a language in which we were all fluent—though we could barely communicate through spoken word. Now it has turned into a global platform for sharing slackline knowledge, history, current competitions, festivals, and big news associated with the sport.

To this day I still chuckle a bit when I hear people I've never met slacklining in a place I've never been, speaking a language I don't speak, calling out the name I gave a trick I made up balancing on a line twenty years ago, stoned in a park while ditching class. It's absolutely outrageous to try to quantify the inspiration you give people or the way your love and energy can alter the trajectory of someone's life, or how much just believing in the impossible can move somebody from halfway around the world. That is, until it happens to you.

I wanted to be the best slackliner in the world and at one point, I held the active free solo world record, the highline world record, and I was the overall international trickline champion in the same year. The value in the effort it took to cumulatively accomplish these feats I never thought could be outdone, but slacklife taught me that inspiration and effort are often circular, and what you value the most in the world is dynamic. Just like most heroes' journeys, there is *katabasis*—a journey through hell, a downfall to which the hero is tested, often beyond their limits, to truly come out stronger on the other side. *Dura duris fraguntur* (Hard things are broken by hard things). The same mindset that led me to greatness almost took my life.

My downright stubbornness to succeed against anything drove me to define myself as a certifiable failure and decimate my self-worth. The blinders I held up to criticism of my dreams being impossible were the same ones that blocked me from hearing anything but praise. The same energy that prided my value in what I did distracted me from ever focusing on who I was or who I wanted to be. I was making the same mistakes over and over again and missing the point. I was losing focus on the journey or worse—I wasn't on it anymore.

In 2015 and 2016, within less than a year, I was challenged with experiencing the greatest losses of my life. I was pushed to my absolute limit with grief, having already lost my best friend, Daniel, and my mentor, Mario, who died in 2013. Then, when Dean died during the most deadly back-to-back season of BASE jumping ever experienced, I became emotionally unstable—maybe for the first time in years I was scared. I became infuriated being a target for criticism. Yet, I put myself up as the target and acted obnoxiously. To feel a sense of control, I often decided to escalate things and make things worse. As if my death had been foreseen, nothing really seemed to matter.

I experienced multiple heartbreaks and lost two of the people I loved most. At one point, I nearly killed myself and my passenger in a car crash, and my life savings barely supported paying the medical bills and other resulting financial necessities of the crash. Rehabbing one of my best friends and lovers for months couldn't have been more painful to endure. My life was only remedied by a GoFundMe campaign, and borrowing $27K from a close friend, Ryan Jenks. But, in the end, I was outrageously in debt, looking at losing my house, in the worst shape physically, mentally, and spiritually since before I slacklined, drinking to excess, partying all the time, and I didn't even have the courage to tell myself I had lost it. Living the lie took me to the edge, and that's where I nearly took my life. Saved by the gods of Hawaii during a Redbull shoot, my friend Alex Mason asked me why I was standing on the railing of the bridge without a parachute. At this point, I couldn't have cared less about my records or my efforts. I didn't even know what I cared about.

My dad once told me, "Time is the greatest teacher, but it kills all its students." Well, records do last forever—they are written in stone—but your record may not be the current record. Times change and with them the records. I worked to break Dean's free solo world record and when I did, he personally congratulated me on progressing the sport. He had also helped get me sponsored and was the one to give me my first-ever packing course for BASE jumping. Rivalry wasn't apparent; it was teamwork if anything. So when Spencer Seabrooke broke my free solo record, I supported him thoroughly, and when Friedi Kühne broke Spencer's record, Spencer showed the exact same sportsmanship.

I can't place anything above the value of Spencer and Friedi being the ones who brought my spirit back to the light from the darkest times I had ever endured. They both got inspired by my energy, enough to work for years to break my record, and then were the ones who showed me the way back to the slacklife I loved—by doing it better than me. Not only by being great slackliners, but also by being good people. My fire was out, but their fire relit me. The same goes for Friedi asking me to write this foreword for his book recently. And during the same time that Spencer was helping me train, it was Friedi live-streaming from his 5,250-foot / 1,600-meter highline attempt, which could have been the highline record at the time. During the first mile, he came super close to sending it before he fell in the end with very strong wind gusts. But he was out there because he loved it, not focusing on the failure but the beauty of where he was and the community that supported him in getting there. Spencer and Friedi, both inspired to break the record I was so obsessed with as well, also ended up being the ones to inspire me back. It was the drive of two people, who may have once seen me as a hero, working hard to eventually be the hero I needed to see. That's slacklife—one part slack, one part life.

Andy Lewis

Prologue

All the crooked paths in my life lead to this narrow line. This is my path, the one I must take, the one I want to take, with all my senses. Every muscle in my body is tense. I hear everything; I see everything; I feel everything. Life couldn't be more intense. Thousands of feelings and thoughts come together to form a deep certainty that I am in the right place here between heaven and earth.

I deliberately exhale loudly and take the next step. Perfection is the only option because only a narrow one-inch band separates me from the fall. Next to me, gigantic masses of water rush into the depths. Thirteen hundred feet / four hundred meters further down they hit rock. One wrong step and the same thing would happen to me. Hunlen Falls, Canada's highest free-falling waterfall, almost hypnotically draws you into the abyss if you look at it for too long. I refocus. A backup? Not available today. I alone hold my life in my own hands. I want it that way. In my opinion, the ultimate, highest form of balancing. The supreme discipline in slacklining, the sport that means everything to me and that has changed my life like nothing else in the world: *free solo.*

* * *

A slackline is a thin, wobbly webbing that you stretch between two trees and then try to balance on. In the perception of many, it is nothing more than a ratchet strap that has been blown up into a trend. Hardly a sport in its own right and certainly not a competitive or extreme sport. And certainly not impressive enough to write an entire book about. Only a typical, spoiled millennial could seriously claim that slacklining is his whole life—and be proud of it.

What can I say? I am that millennial. This narrow webbing is the common thread of my personal story.

On the slackline, I saw the world, made friends, met the love of my life, and, finally, found myself.

Balancing has taught me life lessons, most notably the wonderful liberation of overcoming fear and the importance of setting goals to work toward.

I hope that someone who relives my adventures will have a sparkle in their eyes and perhaps be inspired to overcome their own physical and psychological abysses that appear before each of us every day.

How It All Began

ROSENHEIM
STARTING IN 1994

I grew up near campfires. My childhood was full of wild days, somewhere by a stream bed at the edge of the forest, wrapped in a warm sleeping bag with the smell of smoke in the air and my head in the stars. My father was always thinking of new activities to entice my sister Luise, who was three years younger than me, and me into nature. From scavenger hunts to canoeing tours to makeshift cable cars on which we rushed down the forest slopes of the Jenbach Valley at breakneck speed. Anything to get me, a shy little couch potato, out into the fresh air.

For me, a perfect day consisted of reading comics, watching TV, and building with LEGO® bricks. Nothing with too much physical exertion. Fortunately, my parents always urged me to go hiking or skiing with them. Their latest idea to get me outside was a trampoline for my tenth birthday, on which I spent whole days and half the night, prompting one of the most important steps toward my love for movement through the air.

When we became teenagers and it became cool to do daredevil stunts with our peers, we transferred our crooked somersaults from the trampoline to park benches, walls, and even phone booths. We climbed on everything we could find and jumped off wherever we could. It was called parkour and free running. Explosive, daring, and somehow rebellious.

This is how positive peer pressure had pushed me out into the world, but the little former homebody was—without knowing it—still searching.

Finally, at the age of seventeen, I discovered rock climbing through my classmates Julian and Julius. Less destructive; more in nature. A rush of altitude, a proper strength training session with a great view and with quite a few cool girls who thought the same way. And suddenly, there they were again, the nights in the sleeping bag and by the campfire. I liked that.

But one final dimension of movement through space was still missing.

When I was eighteen, I walked a sixteen-foot / five-meter slackline for the first time during a climbing holiday at Lake Garda.

It was terrible. My legs felt like jelly, and the line just wouldn't stop shaking. No matter how much I waved my arms in the air or tensed my thighs, I always fell over after a few seconds. It drove me crazy.

I said enviously to my friends who were already relatively good at slacklining at the time, "It's not a real sport, it's just a passing trend. So, what do you all want with your stupid slackline?"

How was I supposed to know that this stupid, thin webbing would one day take over my entire life? And yet that is exactly what happened.

My initial frustration gradually turned into defiance. I didn't want to accept that this slackline kept throwing me off. I wanted to be the stronger one; I wanted to conquer this bond; I wanted to show the line who's boss.

And lo and behold: At some point I made progress! Tip toe by tip toe, I approached the other end of the meager campsite line. After hundreds of attempts, I finally managed to walk through my first slackline—and it was a real euphoria. Better than the first somersault on the trampoline and better than reaching the end of a difficult climbing route. Maybe even better than some world records years later.

Suddenly, I was addicted. I wanted more of those feelings of success, that feeling of control, of confidently floating above the ground. I've always had a penchant for excess. When I enjoyed something, I loved it and couldn't get enough of it. When I didn't like something, I detested it. As a little boy, I was constantly building with LEGO® bricks, and later, I spent nights playing computer games, which eventually even cost me my first relationship.

But balancing was different. Here, every minute I devoted myself to this positive addiction was rewarded with more self-confidence and a lasting feeling of happiness. While all the other hobbies I had tried up to that point—from skateboarding to all kinds of musical instruments to soccer and basketball—didn't hold my interest for long, slacklining made me feel for the very first time: "This is my thing. I'll stick to that."

My first highline was over the good old *Wolfsschlucht* (Wolf's Canyon) near Rosenheim, Germany, our hometown, where my friends and I, along with a large group of talented young people, still train regularly today, thirteen years later. Back then, however, it wasn't such a relaxing pleasure. As soon as the abyss opened up beneath me, my body no longer wanted to listen to me. I was drenched in sweat with fear, pale in the face, and couldn't take a single step at this height, even though I could already walk the same distance, about seventy feet / twenty meters, just above the ground.

My friends felt the same way, even the experienced climbers Julian and Julius. But why exactly? In fact, nothing could happen. We were secured, wearing our climbing harness and leash. After every mini-bungee-jump-like fall into the safety rope, of which we had quite a few, we simply had to pull ourselves back up. At least that's usually the case with backups—but more on that later.

So why were we so afraid? Well, this rather novel concept of the safety rope has to be explained to your head first. The mind simply sees an abyss and immediately sets off all the alarm bells. And that's actually a good thing. After all, fear has an evolutionary purpose that goes back millions of years: It warns us and prevents us from taking risks that are too great. At the same time, it mobilizes unimagined forces, whether for defense or escape. Each person's natural primal fears vary in intensity.

For my part, I am terrified of open water or deep diving. The idea of having to swim just thirty feet / ten meters from one boat to another in the open sea or even diving under a boat sends shivers down my spine.

That's exactly how I felt on my first highline.

So, with cool logic, we repeatedly reminded each other that the danger only exists in the mind, and we cheered each other on as much as we could. What always helped me the most were simple, practical tips that more experienced slackliners shouted to me from the edge of the ravine: "Arms up! Look ahead! Bend your knees more!"

And then there were my many self-talks on the line, during which I sometimes even lied to myself: “Everything is fine. Pull yourself together. It’s a completely normal slackline. You are in the park, half a meter above the ground. There is no reason to fall. There is no abyss.”

It took a while, but after many attempts, we finally managed to take the first steps on our first highline. Of course it didn’t just stop at a few steps.

The Inntal Gang

INN VALLEY, BAVARIA, GERMANY
2009–PRESENT

If you want to make progress in slacklining, you can usually only do so by learning from and competing with others. I might have given up on my meager campsite line if I hadn't seen my friends walking effortlessly across it and an inner voice whispering to me, "You'll be able to do that just as well soon. Maybe even better."

I wouldn't be where I am today if I hadn't met many incredibly talented and inspiring people during my slacklining career, some of whom are now my best friends. First and foremost, I would like to mention Alex Schulz, Julian Mittermaier, Lukas Irmler, Valentin Rapp, Pablo Signoret, Mia Noblet, and Spencer Seabrooke, who have always shown me that nothing is impossible on the slackline.

I first met Alex Schulz at Lake Florian near our hometown of Rosenheim. I was about nineteen years old, either just before or after graduating from high school, with only a few months of slacklining experience under my belt, when I spotted something truly extraordinary: Someone had set up a two-hundred-foot-long / sixty-meter-long waterline across the bay! That was gigantic in the slackline world at the time!

I had already balanced waterlines of up to fifty feet / fifteen meters in length but had no idea how to set up such a long line. I also didn't know who would have the material to do this, let alone be able to balance that far.

But Alex was different from my climbing buddies from whom I had learned slacklining. For him, it wasn't just a nice toy to show off. No, he was just as addicted to slacklining as I was. What's more, from the very beginning he had the dream of continuing to balance until he achieved the slackline world record. And for this, he trained passionately and with a plan.

We quickly became friends, and I learned a lot from him, especially about setting up longlines and the complicated handling of pulleys. Even beyond the narrow band, we got along well together and soon went to one or two reggae concerts in Rosenheim and headed off to my first slackline festival together.

The cool thing was that our slackline styles complemented each other wonderfully. Fresh from the trampoline, I was still mainly fixated on tricklining, the variant of slacklining where you do the craziest acrobatic tricks and jumps on a tightly stretched, extra-elastic line. In my early twenties, I dreamed about it constantly. I practiced as much as I could, initially every afternoon after school, then after my community service, and finally after university in the English Garden. The day I landed my first backflip and my first butt bounce on the slackline—both on the same day—was probably the best day of my life at the time.

Alex, on the other hand, simply wanted to balance longer and longer distances, all the way to the slackline world record. He was the ultimate longline talent. And so, at least in the past, we never saw ourselves as competitors.

A few weeks later, through Alex, I met two other great slackline talents while tricklining on the same lake: Valentin Rapp and Julian

Mittermaier. The two are absolute sports enthusiasts. Mountaineering, climbing, skiing, mountain biking, swimming, gymnastics, tennis—there is nothing they haven't done at an advanced level at some point. Not a surprise if you grow up in Brannenburg in the beautiful Inntal, south of Rosenheim. They have always had the mountains on their doorstep and were encouraged by their parents to explore them from an early age. Both are about a year younger than me and are an integral part of my slackline history—just as I am a part of theirs.

If I learned anything from Julian, it's that no slackline should remain free for long. You have to use precious line time. The funny thing is, he says today that he learned the same thing from me. Just like the loud belch of victory at the end of each new highline.

Vale has always been not only a talented slackliner, but he also had an incredible instinct for taking the best photos at a young age and edited our first slackline videos.

It was also through Alex that, while longlining one day, I met the great German slackline personality, the one I was still missing from my circle of friends and from whom I have perhaps learned the most over the years: Lukas Irmler.

The now thirty-six-year-old from Freising was already walking 656-foot-long / 200-meter-long lines in 2011, and that was exactly when I saw him for the first time. Alex and Lukas had set up an 820-foot-long / 250-meter-long line on a meadow in Rosenheim—at that time the polyester slackline world record.

I couldn't even imagine that I would one day be able to balance such distances myself. The line was also kind of scary, tensioned at a height of just six feet / two meters and secured with a heavy chain hoist to more than two tons! This would be unthinkable today, now that we have finally understood that things are easier with less tension! Back then, lines often ripped but, thank God, not that day.

Lukas was an all-rounder. Like me, he took part in trickline competitions, but he was also always an enthusiastic climber. Today he spends almost all his time in the mountains—when he's not doing a handstand on a slackline for a minute. I think it goes without saying that the two of us have often competed with each other, but I don't think that friendly competition has been as beneficial to anyone as it has been to us. For years, we have repeatedly set new world records together or snatched them away from each other in a very short time. And it was Lukas with whom I completed some of my most beautiful, unforgettable highlines.

It was simply a great stroke of luck that we all met at exactly the age when school obligations were coming to an end and one felt the urge to explore the world and prove oneself. Slacklining itself was also still a very young sport, and so it was an absolute rarity to find anyone who took this exotic form of exercise as seriously as we did. This narrow bond immediately connected us more than any football, gymnastics, or music club could ever have achieved.

* * *

In 2012, the entire Inntal Gang gathered at our local mountain, the 6,030-foot-high / 1,838-meter-high Wendelstein, and rigged the Wendelstein Highline for the first time—to this day, a classic among the lines in the Inntal and the location of numerous film and photo shoots. At 230 feet / 70 meters long, it was a new personal record for me and a huge challenge. Stretched to a rigid tension of almost a ton, on heavy, low-stretch polyester, the line was shaking and thrashing around like an eel, just trying to throw you off.

After several attempts, I managed the line on the second day. Alex and Julian had inspired me with how they managed to stay calm on this trembling, wobbling monster, continuously taking one step after another and keeping the line under control with *micro-bounces*. I wanted to do that too.

Eight years later, we added a 1,640-foot-long / 500-meter-long highline to the Wendelstein, within sight of the old 230-foot / 70-meter classic. By traversing the line, we not only set a new German slackline record, but we also had a nostalgic reliving of our beginnings as a team.

Free Solo

Climbing or highlining without safety equipment. Why do people do this? This question can hardly be answered satisfactorily. Most extreme athletes agree: Someone who doesn't do it themself may never be able to understand it.

During my presentations, I sometimes play this team-building game with the audience: You fall backward and are caught by your partner, whom you cannot see. This quickly builds mutual trust.

Free solo highlining is like playing this game with yourself. You let yourself fall, but at the same time stand behind yourself and catch yourself again and again. Who can you trust more than yourself?

But, of course, no slackliner who has always walked with a leash wakes up one day and thinks, "Okay, today I'm going to walk my first free solo highline, preferably 330 feet / 100 meters high." On the contrary, the whole thing is a process that has taken years and started with very small steps. After university, I balanced across the Eisbach river in Munich, first with only the clothes on my back, then with my cell phone in hand, and finally with a backpack full of university documents on my back. Then came higher waterlines, thirty feet / ten meters above the water. An absolutely frightening thought to fall down there, but not fatal. I learned to stay calm despite the pressure. Not because I wanted to set a free solo highline world record one day—you can't plan or predict that—but because it felt good to accept a consequence and trust in my abilities.

As Julian, Lukas, and I got better at highlining and simply stopped falling from short lines, we started playing silly games with our safety: Instead of a climbing harness, we tied the safety rope around our legs, our hands, and our stomachs, a so-called "Swami belt"—these are variations where a fall causes great pain and possible injury, but not death. For non-slackliners, it is important to understand that a fall on a highline does not necessarily mean a fall into the depths. Well-trained slackliners usually hold on to the line with their arms and legs when they lose their balance. I have been training this reflex for years.

* * *

I now want to break up the chronology a bit and anticipate what is probably the most formative adventure of my entire slackline career. This will make all the stages along the way easier to understand.

So off we go for a little detour through a time tunnel to Canada.

My First Free Solo Highline World Record

HUNLEN FALLS, BRITISH COLUMBIA, CANADA
SUMMER 2016

"Dude, I found a spot that's gonna blow your mind," were Spencer's words when he first told me about Hunlen Falls.

"Count me in," was my immediate answer.

Spencer is about my age and lives in British Columbia, Canada. He is nothing less than the perfect embodiment of the freest slackliner life there can be—a fascinating guy who I will introduce in more detail later.

I received the invitation in early 2016, just a few months after Spencer set his free solo highline world record of 210 feet / 64 meters on the Stawamus Chief in Squamish near Vancouver. His enthusiasm for Hunlen Falls, Canada's highest free-falling waterfall, immediately rubbed off on me.

Photos revealed vertical, 1,312-foot-high / 400-meter-high, terrifying dark gray rock walls that gradually turned into a semicircle from the waterfall into an ever-widening, breathtakingly deep gorge. Google Maps told us that we could probably rig several highlines there, from 200 feet / 60 meters to at least 980 feet / 300 meters long, without having to do much climbing or walking. Pure paradise!

And even though I was already in *free solo mode* at that point, I never would have dared to dream what I would do there.

But what does it mean to be in *free solo mode*? Despite still being in the middle of my teacher training, slacklining was my daily routine. I trained on longlines in the park every afternoon during the week and went highlining every weekend and during all semester breaks. At night, before I went to sleep, I was always thinking about the next higher, longer highline.

Outsiders would probably have said that I felt more comfortable on a wobbly ledge at height than on solid ground. So comfortable that I even balanced over it without any safety equipment every now and then. However, there was little evidence of my controversial passion. Unlike today, I avoided spectators, photos, and video recordings of free solo crossings. I just wanted to prove to myself that I could do it and nip any potential outside influence on my ego in the bud.

I only allowed a very few close friends to be there. Among them were Lukas and Vale, who were immediately enthusiastic about the idea of going on a month-long slackline trip to British Columbia during the summer holidays.

So we flew to Vancouver in early August 2016 to meet Spencer, Mia Noblet, and the rest of the SlacklifeBC crew. Mia is a French-Canadian former professional speed skater who, at the age of twenty-one, showed enormous talent for slacklining but still felt relatively uncomfortable on highlines. Today she is one of the best slackliners in the world and has broken the female slackline world record several times, until she finally became the first woman to set a joint record with men. Today, the separate categories no longer exist.

After arriving in Vancouver, we had to drive nearly 560 miles north to reach such a phenomenal location as Hunlen Falls. Once we arrived at Nimpo Lake, the real adventure began. There, we chartered a seaplane from Stewart's Lodge; there are no roads leading to Hunlen Falls. So you have a choice: Either you hike for three days on tiny trails through *Grizzly Country* or you take the shortcut by seaplane.

When you have to lug around over a ton of slackline webbing, ropes, camera and camping gear, this choice isn't exactly difficult. It was my first flight in a seaplane. Actually, it's the same process as with a normal small plane, except that there's no runway underneath you but a lake. When you rush over the water at over 60 mph / 96 km/h just before takeoff, you can't help but admire the technology and the pilot.

It was during the flight that my jaw really dropped. I had used the word *wilderness* several times before but apparently never with any justification until this point. Below us stretched the vastest, loneliest, and most untouched landscape I had ever seen. As soon as Stewart's Lodge disappeared behind us on the horizon, we saw no sign of civilization. Only lakes, swamps, dark green coniferous forests as far as the eye could see and, on the horizon, gigantic mountain ranges whose peaks were still covered in snow.

Spencer and I were lucky enough to sit up front next to the pilot, and we couldn't stop grinning and marveling. The whole thing reached its climax when, after about twenty-five minutes of flight, we spotted a seemingly small, but somehow ever-growing stream in front of us. Before anyone could voice their suspicions, the pilot revealed what we saw in the distance: "That's Hunlen Falls, guys. Take a good look at it."

As the gigantic gorge in front of the waterfall became clearer and clearer, we realized what an incredible location we had arrived at. The roaring waters of Turner Lake plunge 1,312 feet / 400 meters over rugged cliffs into the depths.

While still on the plane, we began to speculate about the possible highlines we would set up there as soon as possible. "The stoke was high," Spencer later said about this moment.

After landing upstream on Turner Lake, which also feeds the falls, and unloading all our gear over a small jetty, we wasted no time setting up camp: Spencer, Michael (whom I had met in Vancouver a year earlier), and I immediately sprinted to the waterfall. While we were walking along a small path in the forest, we passed some signs saying, "Danger! Stay away from the edge!" As we walked past, the roar of the waterfall became louder and louder.

At a small natural viewing platform next to the waterfall, it was so loud that we could barely hear each other, and the air was so humid that everything got wet within seconds.

The view, however, was more than breathtaking. Vast masses of water that abruptly plunge 1,312 feet / 400 meters into the depths from a river that is about 160 feet / 50 meters wide and flows relatively calmly until the last moment. It is a fascinating sight that brutally demonstrates the beautiful yet destructive power of nature. Appearing uniform from a distance, yet chaotic in detail. A demonstration of gravity that almost hypnotically pulls you into the depths.

We carefully crawled on our stomachs to the edge, threw down some stones, and tried to count the time. Without success. After ten seconds, we could no longer see the stones and there was no impact to be heard. That's 1,312 feet / 400 meters of free fall.

Instead, over the roar of the waterfall, another sound became noticeable: the seaplane over 1,000 feet / several hundred meters above us, on its way back to Nimpo Lake. Only when it disappeared over the horizon did we slowly realize how lonely and remote it really was. For the next ten days we would be completely alone with the waterfall. No cell phone reception, no internet.

On the way back to camp, we were much calmer, stayed close together, and talked objectively about our next plans, knowing full well that the pilot had once again emphatically reminded us to take our bear spray with us every time we left camp.

We spent the next few days setting up and climbing three spectacular new highlines: 236 feet / 72 meters long, right in front of the waterfall; 557 feet / 170 meters long, about 330 feet / 100 meters further away; and 885 feet / 270 meters long, about the same distance away.

To set up a slackline over a ravine that cannot be crossed, you first have to fly a fishing line across it using a drone. Then you pull a slightly stronger, usually up to ⅛ inch wide, cord over the fishing line, and then usually the actual slackline. An undertaking that requires teamwork, patience, and trust. Fortunately, we had not only two excellent cameramen, Vale and Levi Allen, but also two experienced drone pilots with us—and so by the evening of the second day, all three of our highlines were already hanging.

It's interesting what altitude does to you. Even if you have walked distances of 230 to 980 feet / 70 to 300 meters several times, it suddenly feels completely different in such a new environment. It makes a difference whether you can see the ground 160 feet / 50 meters below you and orient yourself using clear contours around you, or you are floating 1,300 feet / 400 meters high in the air and can no longer see anything of the ground. When masses of water fall loudly into the depths right next to you, it triggers a serious adrenaline rush even in experienced highliners like Lukas, Spencer, or me—even with safety equipment and the knowledge that nothing can actually happen.

In the evening, around the campfire, we talked about these experiences and made each other more and more excited about the next day. It was also at the campfire that I first felt that here, in this already spectacular place, I wanted to practice what I considered to be the purest and highest form of balancing: a free solo send. Perhaps precisely because it was a place that was frightening.

My personal free solo record up to that point was about 200 feet / 60 meters long at a height of about 160 feet / 50 meters, which meant that the 236-foot / 72-meter line directly in front of the waterfall was within reach. In terms of height and exposure, however, it was a completely different level. I had no idea that it would also be a new world record. For me, it was about doing something big and new in slacklining, something special in a special place that I could be really proud of. And if I am being honest, it was just about satisfying my addiction.

In the following days, after a few crossings of the longer lines, I spent most of my time on the 236-foot / 72-meter highline. I surfed, bounced, and did every trick imaginable. I practiced catching but also threw myself into the leash with full force a few times to put maximum load on the anchor points and see if anything would wobble.

Finally, I walked back and forth on the line several times, slowly, calmly, and with concentration, without any tricks. The latter was rather unusual and immediately caught my friends' attention. "Something was in the air," Lukas said later in an interview.

At some point, Levi came up to me and asked, "Friedi, are you planning to do something special today, and if yes, may I film it?"

The free solo theme was intense for all of us. So much so that, as long as a potential attempt had not yet been decided, we could not talk about it openly. The pressure would have been too much for me, and I still wanted to be 100 percent sure that all the motivation for this endeavor came from within me. But since I was equally aware that a free solo at Hunlen Falls would be real slackline history, and I would regret not having a single picture of it, I allowed my friends to film me—as long as they stayed in the background and I didn't notice anything.

On the fifth day, the time had come. I felt good, properly warmed up but not yet exhausted from all the training. We spent the morning with an intense yoga session on a small jetty by the lake, and during a short meditation, at the end, I began to visualize the upcoming event. I saw myself in front of my closed eyes balancing across the line without any safety equipment, with perfect, smooth movements, without effort, and with a smile on my face.

Then we made our way to the waterfall. After walking back and forth along the line three or four times, I took off my harness without hesitation, said to my friends at the anchor point, "This is it," and began to slide toward the edge of the cliff while sitting on the line.

I had already put some headphones with music in my ears while warming up because I realized that the roar of the waterfall was just too extreme, and I wanted to have a steady rhythm that would carry my even steps over the line. So when I felt comfortable enough, the progressive psytrance music was playing, and I was 100 percent physically and mentally in that moment and place, I stood up and started balancing.

The following ten minutes were certainly among the most intense of my entire life, and yet they passed by in a flash. I was completely in the flow; the past and the future had ceased to exist. Even my ego began to dissolve, almost like a drug high. I consisted only of my steady breathing and the interplay between the vibrations of the line and my soft balancing movements.

I walked much slower than with the safety harness, but I still kept putting one foot in front of the other. Without thinking too much about it, I had gotten past the middle when a small break in my flow became apparent. I knew from previous ascents that the last quarter, the few feet just before the opposite edge, would be the hardest for me. That's when I often fell on longer, more technically demanding lines—when the end was within reach. So I forced myself to walk even slower and more carefully.

I began to repeat my inner mental mantra, "You just started walking. Every step is like the first. You will move on. You have control over the slackline. It can't throw you off. You've walked much harder lines before. . . ."

My walk did indeed become a little shaky toward the end, but I didn't let it deter me, and my regular breathing carried me through the difficult moments. The flow was back.

Suddenly, without realizing it, I was balancing over the edge, had forest floor beneath my feet again, and six feet / two meters in front of me was the tree where the slackline ended. Slowly and carefully, I crouched down and stepped off the line. Only when my feet touched the ground did the most intense, animalistic, and honest scream of joy I had ever uttered before burst out of me.

I was flooded with euphoria and gratitude for being alive, for being in this place, for being able to be myself. No video game, no movie, no comic, and no book can convey such an intensity of life energy or even evoke a hint of it. Goodbye couch potatoes.

I had done it. Not only was this the world's longest free solo highline ascent and by far the longest of all unsecured records, but it was also the first time I had someone film me during a free solo walk.

At the evening campfire, I realized how important this discipline had become to me and how much my friends had trusted in me. And above all, how much I had trusted in myself. When Spencer finally happily acknowledged that the length of 236 feet / 72 meters had indeed beaten his old world record, I finally made the decision to tell my slackline world about it.

The following chapters are dedicated to this slackline world and my journey through it.

So back through the time tunnel to 2014, when I still identified myself primarily as a trickliner and didn't even dare to dream of highline world records.

THE WEST

The Year Abroad

PORTLAND, OREGON, USA
2015

The Arrival

On August 25, 2014, one of the greatest adventures of my life began. I had ten months ahead of me in Portland, Oregon, where I would work as an assistant teacher at Lewis & Clark College. Portland is considered the *weirdest* city on the West Coast and is, among other things, the home of *The Simpsons* writer Matt Groening, who named many of his yellow characters after Portland streets.

I had never been to the US before, nor had I been away from home for such a long time in a place where I didn't know anyone. . . . I was super nervous. When I was on the last leg of the flight from Seattle to Portland, the flight attendant at the gate asked if I would like to sit by the window, and her colleague answered for me, "Oh yeah, give him a window seat. Just look at him, this guy wants to fly." I became more and more convinced that I was in for a great time.

During my first few days on campus, I was so busy and had so much to discover that I didn't have any time to be homesick or excited. On the third day, I started teaching my own German courses.

But, of course, the highest priority for leisure activities remained—slacklining. I quickly found some like-minded students who could at least walk a few steps on the line and started to tell their friends about the "crazy German language assistant who does backflips on a slackline."

Smith Rock

Smith Rock is a ridge of orange-brown rock formations that rise several thousand feet / several hundred meters out of the Central Oregon High Desert. The state park is not only one of the largest climbing meccas on the American West Coast, but it has also been an extremely popular destination for highliners for almost twenty years. At the Highline Festival, which has been taking place annually since 2012, locals and slackliners from all over the West Coast come together to balance through the air between the iconic rock formations.

In September 2014, when I had only been in the US for ten days, the festival was just around the corner, and I really wanted to be there. I was pretty nervous because I didn't know anyone there and had no idea what a slackline festival was like in the US. But the fear of missing out was much greater.

I found a ride at the last minute and found myself back at the location a short time later. As I was walking aimlessly and shyly through the state park parking lot on Saturday morning, I met none other than Jerry Miszewski, the former highline world record holder (2011–2012) and founder and owner of Balance Community, my current slackline sponsor.

I was in awe and lucky to arrive just in time to walk with Jerry up to his highline, "Temple of the Winds." Only today do I truly realize how important it was to me back then to impress him.

I then struggled across the slackline, which was incredibly shaken by the wind, and was one of only three slackliners at the entire festival who was able to master the 236-foot / 72-meter distance.

Word got around quickly. The German kid had entered the scene. . . .

Work Hard, Play Hard

In the evening, all the slackliners met in nearby Terrebonne at a western-themed cowboy ranch to celebrate their highline experiences together. At the grill stood a cheerfully grinning guy with a black three-day beard and skater clothes. He distributed thick burger patties and stirred vigorously every few minutes in a huge pot of steaming chili con carne.

When it was my turn, he greeted me with the words, "How's it going, buddy? What's your name?"

I replied shyly with my unmistakable German accent, "Hi. I'm Friedi. How are you, and what's your name?"

"Friedi? Are you the crazy slackliner from Germany? My name is Ari. I saw you killing it on the Kingline today."

"I am from Germany, yes. Nice to meet you, Ari. I'm very glad to be here."

"Well, it's a pleasure to have you here, Friedi! How do you want your burger?"

That's how I met Ari DeLashmutt, a twenty-seven-year-old Central Oregon local, self-proclaimed anarchist, and former professional skier, bursting with *joie de vivre*. We quickly became friends because our motto seemed to be the same: "Get the most fun possible out of every single day." That meant the following for this and all our upcoming weekends in Smith Rock: The narrow access paths to the highlines will not be hiked but sprinted—no matter how hot the sun is from the sky. Everything up to the fourth difficulty level is climbed free solo because climbing ropes only slow you down unnecessarily. On the descent, you half jump and half slide over scree fields. As soon as a highline is free, people jump on it. And above all: Danger is not discussed at length but laughed at loudly in the face. So on the last day of the festival, he gave me the nickname "Speedy Friedi."

But back to the party: At first, I was a bit hesitant as I moved from one conversation to the next. I was the only foreigner at the festival and yet I didn't feel a bit strange. I hadn't even been in the US for two weeks yet and hadn't met any of the people there until that day; yet, I was immediately able to have a brilliant conversation with them. They were all slackliners, mostly only a few years older than me at the tender age of twenty-four. An American friend of mine—I don't remember which one—later called this group of people "redneck hippies." And that hit the nail on the head. Torn jeans, old lumberjack shirts, and worn-out sandals, long hair, the boys all unshaven, tanned skin, wiry physiques, and always a radiant smile on their faces. This gave the look of a typical West Coast slackliner, both for the boys and the girls.

That evening, I also met Spencer Seabrooke, whom I briefly introduced during the Hunlen Falls free solo adventure. He wasn't wearing any of the abovementioned clothes because he was sitting in a hot tub the whole time.

I could swear that Spencer was sitting in a homemade *hillbilly hot tub* with his arm around a beautiful woman wearing only a bikini on both his left and right. In one hand he held a beer, in the other hand a thick, smoking joint.

Someone said to me, "That's Spencer Seabrooke, the guy who almost died free soloing. He's crazy." Or something like that.

Many would probably describe Spencer's lifestyle as "sex, drugs, and rock'n'roll." He calls it simply "slacklife."

The fact is: The now thirty-four-year-old Canadian lives in his van and works on construction sites just enough to be able to afford to drive around North America and have adventures the rest of the year. He has a zest for life like hardly anyone else I have met on my travels.

Of course we didn't become best friends overnight. We first had to sniff each other out like two skeptical dogs, both with the claim to be alpha animals. The grinning look he gave me from the hot tub read something like this: "So you're the German kid that everyone talks about and who's supposed to kick ass on the line, huh? I'll believe it when I see it."

For me, back then, it was all about pure athletic ability. Who can balance further than me? Who can surf the line harder? Who never needs the safety leash?

In this respect, Spencer was still behind me, but he made up for it with an almost superhuman motivation and strength and, to use his own jargon, "the biggest balls around."

Without knowing it at the time, these brief but intense encounters laid the foundation for countless formative adventures in the US and some of my closest international friendships.

American College Life

In addition to those who were already irreversibly infected, I was also able to infect some students with the balance virus in the following period. My friend Atsatsa, the only Native American at Lewis & Clark College, founded the first slackline club there, which, thanks to generous financial support from the college, was soon able to purchase its own longline and highline equipment. The twenty-year-old member of the Navajo Nation has a truly phenomenal sense of balance and no fear of heights. To this day, I have never seen anyone make such rapid progress in slacklining. My wish and promise to one day do a highline event with him in his hometown of Arizona are still rock solid.

During my first few weeks in the US, I also came to the realization that boozy college parties, as seen in movies, were by no means just a stereotype but reality. With scantily clad dancing teenagers, lots of cheap beer from a funnel or from shotgunning, thick white clouds of smoke, sometimes bouncy gangsta rap, and sometimes live concerts by shaggy-haired college rock bands. And afterward, you usually end up with a completely devastated college dorm room or a parents' house that desperately needs renovations.

I once witnessed such a house party being busted. Suddenly the music stopped, and the twenty-year-old host ran from room to room shouting, "This party is over, get the fuck out of my house!"

Just a few minutes later, the police arrived, and I watched from the street as several stern-looking officers with flashlights went into the house and questioned the youths who hadn't made it out in time for their personal details. Of course alcohol was only allowed here from the age of twenty-one, and noise pollution in general was just as unacceptable as it was back home.

We just wanted to get away. My bad luck was that the taxi that Atsatsa, a few friends, and I wanted to use to escape was already completely full. Atatsa looked at the taxi driver and nodded toward the trunk. The driver nodded in the same direction: "Just hop in, man."

While the police were standing less than thirty feet / ten meters away from us, cleaning up a party, Speedy Friedi was supposed to jump into the escape trunk. Then it dawned on me: I had become a character in an American college teen comedy.

Time Flies

My insatiable hunger for new, longer lines, coupled with the openness and cleverness of my new American friends, resulted in many first highline ascents in the months following the Smith Rock Festival.

With Ari, I was soon balancing over canyons in Central Oregon. With Joel Pinnock—another acquaintance from Smith Rock—and Atsatsa, I walked what was then Oregon's longest highline over the Punch Bowl Falls.

At the annual THC—The Humboldt Classic, a slackline festival in Humboldt County, Northern California—I balanced through a primeval forest between enormous redwoods and giant sequoia trees, while thick white clouds of smoke from California marijuana rose below me. Not only did I get to know the Californian hippie slackline scene, but I also reconnected with my childhood in a crazy way: It was in this very forest that the forest moon Endor scenes in *Star Wars: Return of the Jedi*, my favorite film of my childhood, were filmed.

It was a dream: I was balancing through the air where Luke and Leah Skywalker had (or will have?) lightsaber battles and hoverbike races with the Empire.

My first winter without snow had its ups and downs. While attempting a butt flip on a trickline that was far too high and far too tight at the world-famous Santa Monica Beach in Los Angeles, I slipped off the line so badly that it shot up and severely sprained my wrist. After that, I was finally fed up with tricklining and wanted to concentrate fully on highlining.

A week later, I was in a much better mood as I found myself on my first highline in Hawaii over palm jungle and lava rock.

In the spring, I went deep into the Enchantments, a picturesque mountain range in eastern Washington State, with Carl Marrs and Ben Plotkin-Swing, whom I had also met at Smith Rock, where we rigged a 390-foot-long / 120-meter-long alpine highline—at the time the longest in the entire state. These guys were both pillars and competitors in a positive sense. We encouraged each other to hike faster, carry heavier backpacks, balance higher and further, and be less afraid.

Ben, who was also twenty-five at the time, was in many ways a kind of antithesis to Spencer. A quiet, thoughtful nerd who enjoyed the perfectly planned construction of a highline far more than any party afterward. Today he has a doctorate in physics, but back then he was one of the strongest highliners in North America.

Once, Ben was able to complete a new line that I couldn't even manage after two days of trying: a 390-foot-long / 120-meter-long line on an old railway bridge somewhere on the eastern outskirts of Seattle. I was very envious of Ben for this, even a little angry with him inside, trying to blame the weather conditions for his success and my failure . . . but the fact is, he was simply better than me that day. And envy doesn't get you anywhere, I even wrote that in my diary back then. But we do encourage each other and are happy for each other. Just like at home with Juli, Lukas, Alex, and co.

Hitchhiking Through the Wild West? Not a Chance.

At the end of that very frustrating weekend, Ben took me to a gas station near the southbound highway entrance. I had the whole evening and night to hitchhike the 190 miles from Seattle to Portland.

For three hours, I stood on the side of the road, smiling as kindly as I could and holding my thumb up in the air. Hundreds of cars rushed past me, almost all without passengers and with tons of space in the huge vehicles. But no one stopped or slowed down even a bit when they saw me. Some even accelerated.

I forced myself to keep smiling, but soon it became cold and dark. The cardboard sign I made at the gas station that said "Toward Portland" didn't help, nor did my now pleading looks. I thought about my family, my childhood bedroom, my home. The regulated processes. Even the lecture halls. Everything that had ever given me security and safety. For the first time, I felt truly homesick and began to cry. Hitchhiking could hardly be more counterproductive.

At some point I got over my fear and called Ben, who had already been skeptical about my *unrealistic* plan. He was now with his girlfriend's family north of Seattle, so he couldn't pick me up, but he gave me perfect instructions over the phone on how to take the bus to his shared apartment. At that time, I still didn't have a smartphone with internet.

On the bus, I noticed the many tired, worn-out people who were driving home from work at ten o'clock in the evening with glazed-over eyes. Quite a few seemed mentally absent, numbed by alcohol or worse. Public transportation in the US was obviously for those who couldn't afford a car.

In the city center, I saw skyscrapers, homeless people, rich people, and a Michael Brown demonstration and memorial procession with banners: "This is not a game," "End police violence," and "Fuck the police."

When I finally arrived at Ben's apartment, it was after midnight—my bus to Portland left at 5:30 the next morning. Since I couldn't charge my phone to set an alarm due to a lack of an adapter, I used an old Native American tactic: I drank so much water before going to bed that I was guaranteed to wake up in a few hours from the pressure in my bladder.

It worked.

On the bus to Portland, I thought about how incredibly versatile the word *adventure* can be. It was still my favorite word.

Sunday, 2/22/2015

Spencer, Ari, and I run through Smith Rock Park toward the highlines. At the foot of the wall, a gigantic adrenaline rush begins. My first free solo multi-pitch climb.

Ari assured me again and again how easy the route was, how stable the rock was, and how much of the danger was only in my head. He knows exactly where to climb and where to rest.

Spencer: "I've done it before, too, dude. It's a walk in the park."

So we start climbing. First Ari, then me, then Spencer. Soon we even overtake two secured rope teams. Name of the route: Super Slab, difficulty: 5.8, on the European scale between 5 and 5+. Absolutely doable and no reason for me to fall, but still quite a thrill without a rope 50, 80, at some points 100 meters [160, 260, and 330 feet] above the ground.

Ari tells the story afterward like this: "I get to the top after the final moves, and I can't see Friedi or Spencer yet because they are behind a corner, but I hear Friedi screaming, 'ARI!... ARI!' and I'm like 'Oh crap, Friedi needs help now,' but then Friedi goes, 'ARI!!! I'M HAVING SO MUCH FUN!! THIS IS AWESOME!'"

As we sit on the rock in the evening sun after our highline session, gazing out over Smith Rock State Park, I ask Spencer what he does with his life.

"I do physical work at construction sites for a living. But I smoke joints at work all day, dude. It's just more fun that way."

When I asked him if he smokes weed before highlining, he answered with a grin, "Is a duck's ass watertight?" – Canadian slang for "Of course."

Somehow Spencer reminds me of the older guys from the sports field scene in my hometown of Kolbermoor. At first glance, he seems like a macho and a braggart, but the better you get to know him, the more likable he becomes. Unlike most loud people, his self-confidence is genuine and well-founded. And it's almost impossible to be in a bad mood in his presence. There's just too much to laugh about with him.

My First Trip to Spencer's Hood

In early April 2015, I had a ride from Portland to Seattle to see Joel. The driver, a mid-forty-year-old man named Jason, was somehow creepy. He constantly complained about the government (which in itself is not a reason for me to dislike him) and blamed dark conspiratorial forces for his personal misery.

"The mechanic intentionally fucked up my car, the Jews control everything, women are all the same. . . ."

All right, I thought to myself, silently hoping that the car ride would pass quickly. He was constantly yelling at other drivers, and when we couldn't find Joel's house right away, he had a fit of rage and shouted, "Get the fuck out of my car. Right now."

Relieved, but unfortunately still without a smartphone, I got out and walked around aimlessly for a while until Joel finally found me and picked me up. A short time later, we were sitting in his small car and on our way to British Columbia.

After a late arrival and a night in a roadside tent, we awoke at the base of Stawamus Chief in Squamish, an hour north of Vancouver. At 2,300 feet / 700 meters high, the Chief is one of the largest granite monoliths in the world and the Canadian climbing and highlining paradise par excellence.

A little later, Carl, Ben, Joel, Spencer, and I climbed the mountain, highly motivated and carrying 66-pound / 30-kilogram backpacks. After about ninety minutes of panting and sweating, we finally stood at the 980-foot-deep / 300-meter-deep gorge that runs through the granite giant.

Spencer answered the question of how to get the connecting rope across with a skillful shot from his "Lucky Launcher," a harpoon powered by air pressure. This device, originally designed for rescue purposes, fires an arrow with a string up to 230 feet / 70 meters.

So we rigged Spencer's 210-foot / 64-meter home line and future free solo line, "Itus," and the new 330-foot / 101-meter highline, "Pandemic," which Ben had drilled flawlessly months earlier. Both lines have incredible quality. Over 820 feet / 250 meters high, at perfect 90° angles away from the vertical rock.

Ben and I each crossed the new line with several catches. It wasn't easy to walk that line. I balanced the shorter one back and forth several times and enjoyed the air beneath me. A quiet evening around the campfire with Carl, Ben, and Joel followed, while Spencer walked down the mountain to spend the night in his van with a date. What a starry sky lay above us!

Sunday, 4/5/2015

Ben hesitates until noon before trying "Pandemic" for the first time. I'm not allowed on it before then. Even after his first attempts with a few falls, he doesn't want me to try it: "It's my project, it was my effort, I should get the first ascent...."

I see how much pressure he's putting on himself, how nervous the line is making him. We talk about it at length—and it's really good for both of us and ultimately leads him to the conclusion that he was hypocritical and that we should support each other as much as possible.

An hour later, I succeed in completing the first complete send of Canada's longest highline. I don't think I'm a technically stronger walker than Ben at the moment. But on the one hand, I put in more attempts and, on the other hand, unlike last time, I put less pressure on myself than he did. After my broadcast, everyone congratulates me except Ben. He probably still has to digest it a bit, but "What doesn't kill you makes you stronger" doesn't just apply to the body. Even the ego needs to take a hit every now and then in order to grow.

Then, after many attempts, he finally manages to walk the line from anchor to anchor. He should be celebrating after all the pressure, but he's rather quietly and secretly happy.

To celebrate the day, I finally let Spencer persuade me to eat one of his triple infused weed brownies. After about forty-five minutes, it kicks in. I start seeing strange LEGO®-like

```
figures in the campfire, hear the blood pounding
in my ears, get a slight fear of the 300-meter-
high [980 foot-high] cliff that is only 15 meters
[50 feet] away from our campfire, and can no
longer articulate myself properly. This is too
much. Thank goodness the sleeping bag is right
next to me. The night is clear, and my body is
completely exhausted. So, off to bed.
```

Farewell

My time as a language assistant at Lewis & Clark College was coming to an end, which made me very sad. On the last evening, I met with the other foreign language assistants from France, Russia, Spain, China, and Japan. At a fancy campfire on a rooftop terrace in downtown Portland, we had a long chat about the past ten months. I realized that I never had a particularly deep connection with them. I guess I always seemed a bit strange to them, with my clothes worn out from climbing and my stories of crazy adventures.

I felt a little sorry that they didn't have a slackline community. I was just incredibly lucky. All my experiences were almost served to me on a silver platter. For me, America was hardly a culture shock. What must it have been like for Chu-Yen from China, for example? At least I got a two-week visit from my father and had the slackline community. She had neither.

Who had shown more courage and strength in the last ten months? I think she did.

The Place Where It All Began

YOSEMITE NATIONAL PARK, CALIFORNIA, USA
2015

After a tearful farewell, Joel picked me up from campus. On the long drive to central California, we once again discussed politics and the differences between America and Europe.

"George Bush was the worst president we ever had," he said.

With a clairvoyant grin, I replied, "You mean the worst president you had SO FAR."

So the time passed quickly. When we finally passed through the entrance to the promised Yosemite Valley, we were speechless.

"Our jaws dropped to the floor and through the floor of the car into the road."—Joel Pinnock

It was the most epic sight I had ever seen. And that continues to this day. Yosemite is like a painting: dark green coniferous forests and crystal-clear lakes and rivers, surrounded by majestic mountains whose snow-capped peaks provide the meltwater in summer for numerous waterfalls that cascade down the steep, gray rock walls into the valley. A fairytale landscape, rightly protected and safeguarded with all the means at the state's disposal.

We drove straight to the original Camp 4, where climbers invented slacklining almost fifty years earlier. During their rest days in the late 1970s, they balanced first on chains and ropes and then on flat nylon belts, playfully training their balance and coordination whenever their arms and fingers needed a break from climbing.

Slackline icons such as Scott Balcom and Dean Potter soon began to take the balancing sport up into the air, first, stretching the rope from treetop to treetop and finally, between rock towers and over ravines. Dean Potter, a professional climber and BASE jumper who practically called Yosemite home his entire life, was one of the first people to walk on highlines without safety equipment.

Saturday, 5/9/2015

A freakish four-hour climb over steep, rocky trails to Upper Yosemite Falls with Joel, Jerry, Ryan, Garrison (sixteen years old!), Justin, and his ice-blue-eyed husky Bishop.

It's worth it: We rig three epic, picturesque, exposed, *real* highlines, just as they should be. They exceed the height in Squamish by almost 200 meters[660 feet].

Jerry is tired and allows me to make my first attempt on the "Big Big Yosemite Falls Line," which at the time was the longest highline in the entire valley at 113 meters [370 feet]. All the training is finally paying off, and I am walking OS FM FA (Onsight Full Man First Ascent).

But the shorter "Big Yosemite Falls Line," the 70-meter-long [230-foot-long] classic, is even better. It is very exposed; you walk right up to the edge of the waterfall, feel the updrafts, and have 500 meters [1,640 feet] of air beneath your feet all the way to the ground. Perhaps the most beautiful highline I've been on so far.

I walked it *continuous full man* with surfing, bouncing, exposure turns with side-sag, and leaning into the wind. I feel the progress I have made since coming to America.

Divine evening by the campfire, under a divine starry sky, with lots of laughter and divine conversations. One difference from Squamish: Here you absolutely have to lock away all your supplies in bear cans and hang them on trees at night because there are very clever brown bears in Yosemite.

Ryan: "Guys, did you know there is a bear in this mountain, a very clever female one, who learned to carry the bear canisters to the top of a cliff, push them down, and then go to the bottom to pick the food from the broken containers?"

Before going to bed, we take a night hike to the nearby Lost Arrow Spire, possibly the most famous highline spot in the world. We see the gigantic, 100-meter-high [330-foot-high] rock needle 20 meters [70 feet] on the other side of the cliff in the light of our headlamps. The whole location inspires respect and has something historic, something grand about it. This is where Scott Balcom walked the first highline ever in 1985. The 15-meter [50-feet] "Classic Line." A place steeped in history that everyone who calls themselves a highliner dreams of at some point. I decide that I have to come back here and walk this line.

Two days later, most of our group said goodbye. Only Joel and I remained. We went highlining for two more days on the other side of the valley, at Taft Point Lookout, a much easier-to-reach spot. We enjoyed the peace, the view, and the wilderness around us. The biggest thrill for us was crossing the 100-foot-long / 30-meter-long and 1,640-foot-high / 500-meter-high line at night and plunging into the leash in almost complete darkness.

After that, we had enough of balancing and wanted to devote ourselves to climbing.

Joel had already checked into Camp 4 before me, but it was now packed. And so my very own, somewhat different Yosemite adventure began. . . .

* * *

My first mistake:

I politely ask the ranger at the reception if I might be able to stay at Joel's campsite for an additional charge.

Their answer: "When the sign says Camp 4 is full, it is full. If we still find you here in half an hour, it will be a problem for you."

They don't care that I don't have a car to get anywhere else. So this is how far my honesty has brought me. I guess I have no choice but to camp somewhere wild.

My second mistake:

As I started walking toward the forest with my sleeping bag on my back, the rangers must have seen me from the parking lot. With my weak headlamp, I stumble through the undergrowth. Because of disgusting worms on the ground, I look for a place to sleep on a thirteen-foot-high / four-meter-high boulder, on a narrow, almost horizontal ledge, just wide enough so that I don't slide off while lying down.

As soon as I roll out my small sleeping mat, I see huge flashlights coming toward me through the trees in the distance. My heart sinks into my pants. It must be the rangers. At the very top of the rock, I duck behind a ledge on the other side of the lights and hold on with my fingers to avoid slipping. So only my fingertips are on the side of the rock facing the rangers. I turned off my headlamp long ago.

They are getting closer and closer. I hear their murmuring, but I can't understand what they're saying. The beams of the flashlights sweep over everything around me but mostly search the ground. They also briefly brush over my hands. My heart is racing.

I'm lucky they don't see me and, for some reason, they don't see my sleeping bag either, which is still on the ledge on the other side. I imagine what would have happened if they had found me. They probably would have tried to hold me down, overpower me, maybe even handcuff me. At the very least, they would have thrown me out of the park, perhaps reported me, or imposed a fine. Possibly banishing me forever from the place I had just come to love so much. . . .

The adrenaline rushes through my veins. The feeling surpasses any fear of getting caught I've ever had. As a child, I was excited by playing hide-and-seek, by ringing doorbells, by taking unauthorized trips to neighbors' gardens . . . it was all a joke. Copying from the student next to you at school, staying out later than allowed, nightlife with a fake student ID . . . all for free. Now I am twenty-five years old and about to be arrested in the US of all places. No more games.

I cling to the rock grimly and remain there for twenty minutes without moving. The rangers are gone. Their lights disappeared.

As I begin to prepare my sleeping quarters, I see light again, this time from the opposite direction. Same procedure, same adrenaline rush. I dare to take a look and this time I quickly realize that they are not rangers, but just a single person, also with a headlamp. Probably a climber looking for a stealth campsite, just like me. He stays well away from me, doesn't see me, and finally disappears back into the forest.

The sleeping space on the edge is tight, but good enough. My heart is still racing so fast that it takes me over an hour to fall asleep.

My phone wakes me up at 6 a.m. and I sneak around Camp 4 in a wide arc to go back to the reception from the side of the road.

* * *

Finally, an official campsite became available, and I was able to check in.

Sunday, 5/17/2015

Helicopters circle over the valley. The mood in the camp is depressed, something is in the air. We learn that the previous evening, Dean Potter and his friend Graham Hunt had a fatal accident while wingsuit BASE jumping. They wanted to fly right through the narrow gulley that we had seen from the Taft Point Exit two days earlier. It was immediately clear to us that it would be very difficult to fly through there. It is probably doable but very challenging.

We spent the last few days in the valley climbing: lots of hard cracks, sport climbing routes rated way too easy, and some easier slab multi-pitch climbs, which we even did without a rope. We sneaked into the more upscale housekeeping campsite a few times to use the showers there. I once even walked into the $700-a-night Ahwahnee luxury hotel to use the Wi-Fi. Anything is possible if you radiate self-confidence and appear totally relaxed and carefree.

So I was able to plan my last trip to North America between climbing and slacklining. My work visa was about to expire, so I had to leave the States. Back home in Germany, however, university would not resume until four months later.

So what could be more natural than paying a final visit to the US's northern neighbor and then flying home from there?

Canadian Slacklife

SQUAMISH, BRITISH COLUMBIA, CANADA
2015

Saturday, 6/6/2015

Spencer, Michael, and I are rigging the 30-meter-long [100-foot-long] "Dean's Line" on the Stawamus Chief in memory of Dean Potter, who first walked this line many years ago and passed away three weeks ago.

Also, a new 90-meter [300-foot] line that no one has sent yet. After I walk the line for the first time, singing the entire *Fresh Prince of Bel-Air* intro to myself, Spencer suggests, "Let's call this line 'The Fresh Prince.'"

We are joined by several Vancouver Slack hippies: Andrew, Levi, RJ, Lee, Hanna, John, Matt, Keenan, Ryan, Hiko, Johannes, Jonas, Richard, Amanda, Garika, Brent. They are setting up another 20-meter [70-foot] line.

Spencer and I hang upside down by our feet—he on the 30-meter line, me on the 20-meter—and

```
play Rock, Paper, Whippers: like Rock, Paper,
Scissors, but the loser has to drop into the
safety device. Laughter.
Afterward, everyone dances to Bob Marley in the
sun on the cliff.
```

Quit While You're Ahead

After three days on the Chief, we went back down to Squamish to recharge our batteries with some Canadian energy: After a Mountain Man Breakfast—hash browns, three fried eggs, bacon, ham, tomato, cantaloupe, buttered toast, and two pancakes with maple syrup—we went waterlining across the wonderfully crystal-clear Brohm Lake. Levi Allen accompanied me with his drone as I walked my longest waterline to date, 430 feet / 130 meters, sixteen feet / five meters above the water glittering in the sunlight.

There was no rest the next day either. At the nearby 230-foot-high / 80-meter-high waterfall known as Brandywine Falls, we rigged a highline that was as long as it was high. It was Spencer's longest course yet and he fought like an animal. Michael and I were thrilled with his every move. When Spencer finally managed to walk his new personal best distance after numerous catches and leash falls, we all burst into cheers. Never before have I been so happy for someone else while slacklining. I felt his euphoria, as if I had just conquered a gigantic line myself.

A month later, Spencer returned to celebrate his personal record: He tied himself to the highline with a long rope and rode down the waterfall in an inflatable boat, with a Canadian flag fluttering behind him as a Superman cape. All of these scenes can be seen in Levi Allen's adventure documentary *Untethered*.

No sooner were these two wannabe rest days over than my last big slackline goal in Canada called us back to the Chief. We converted the remaining 300-foot / 90-meter line into a new 440-foot / 135-meter line. The longest in all of Canada to date.

This time, I was not up to the challenge. On my first attempt on the heavy band with backup loops that were sometimes too tight, I didn't even get to the middle. My body was screaming for a break.

The next day things weren't any better. I felt like a dead battery and burned my last reserves of energy with numerous catches and leash falls on the much-too-wobbly tread. It was like balancing on a giant sleeping dragon that would wake up at the slightest wrong move and start throwing you off with powerful thrusts. Then the rain came.

Half an hour later, Spencer, Michael, and I were sitting under a makeshift tarp camp, smoking joints and eating whatever snacks we could get our hands on. As long as the fire burned, it remained somehow cozy. By the time Michael and I were crying our eyes out with laughter because Spencer was so high that he turned into a little kid and started rolling and jumping around in his sleeping bag, I realized that highlining wasn't everything in life.

By the third day I was just mud. The rain had turned into fog, so that on my last attempt on the monster line I could not see more than seventy feet / twenty meters and could walk even less. Spencer sat at the anchor behind me and watched me with a grin. He would probably have stayed up there with me forever. Until I had done it.

But at some point, you have to admit defeat. So we packed up, sprinted down the Chief one last time, took one last swim in the icy mountain stream below, and cruised back to Vancouver on the Sea to Sky Highway in the sunset.

Sunday, 6/21/2015

My last night in Canada

Summer Solstice party in the woods in a rustic mountain cabin with a space net in front of it, which Spencer, Michael, and I rigged between the trees with ratchet lines.

Seven meters [twenty-three feet] above the forest floor, Spencer and I simultaneously free solo the lines to the net hanging in the middle and drop into it with a high five.

The DJ plays groovy deep house music on a huge sound system in front of the forest hut. The three of us climb a 60-meter-high [200-foot-high] tree until we see the lights of Vancouver.

Endless laughter fits.

The DJ does a backflip, hits a piece of glass in his hand as he lands, and bleeds all over. He is taken to the hospital by his girlfriend and stitched up. Two hours later he continues playing.

```
Disco balls and disco lights make the canopy
above around fifty dancing hippies shimmer and
glitter.
The rest are blurry memories.
```

The following day, at the airport, I wrote the last words in my diary, in tears: “The best ten months of my life.”

Leveling Up: The Gate of the Worlds

WILDER KAISER, AUSTRIA
2015

Back home, I was pleased to see that the Inntal Gang hadn't grown apart at all despite my ten-month absence. Vale, Juli, and Lukas were still just as crazy about highlining as I was, and we still got along great. This was especially evident during our personal slackline milestone in the summer of 2015.

We went to the Wilder Kaiser Mountains in Austria to set up a 230-foot-long / 70-meter-long true alpine masterpiece above *Kleines Törl* (little gate). Six thousand five hundred sixty feet / two thousand meters above the valley, surrounded by gray, rugged rocks and often above the clouds.

After an ascent of almost 4,922 feet / 1,500 meters, laden with heavy backpacks, we gratefully slept one night at the Fritz Pflaum Hut. Although you can hardly call it a full night if you get up at three in the morning. But when you have as much planned as we do, there is no other way. We climbed another 1,640 feet / 500 meters to the Kopftörlgrat as the sun slowly rose over the Alps—and then the real adventure began: climbing, rappelling, partner work on the rock face, setting up a highline. . . .

* * *

Lukas and Juli are the stronger climbers and, therefore, take on the more difficult tour on the eastern side of the ridge. Vale and I form the second rope team on the other side, with slightly easier climbing, but still not without its challenges. The bolt spacing on the routes is large, up to about thirty feet / ten meters, so we use friends and nuts where possible to secure ourselves. Again and again, we have to climb detours to pull the tagline that connects us to the other side up past all the sharp rocks.

After several hours of alternating between freezing and sweating, waiting for others and pulling on ropes, the ultimate mood killer comes: One of the many thick clouds of fog that repeatedly move through the ridge gets stuck right next to us.

Within a few minutes, we can no longer see the other side. Super. All that effort and then this. We wait for a while, but the visibility doesn't improve. Finally, we make the decision together to try it anyway. It's already early afternoon, and all four of us want to go up the line at least once more, dismantle it, and descend back down to the valley.

Juli makes the first attempt—it is the first time in years that I have witnessed him fail to complete a highline on his first try. With a few catches he fights his way to the other side. Meanwhile, the clouds have loosened up a little and we can see the other side for a few seconds before it closes in again just as quickly.

Nevertheless, Juli manages to cross the line on the way back. Thank God! This means that it has been walked for the first time. And by Juli, who had the idea for the project. That's how it should be.

We're happy, but it's not a full celebration just yet. Lukas and I are pretty nervous; we really want to walk the line too.

Two hundred thirty feet / seventy meters is well within our capabilities, but given today's conditions, we have real doubts. Especially since you can never access the full potential of your strength after a mountain tour.

"Crazy shit, much harder than expected. I thought I could just walk over there, but I had to fight quite a bit. Make sure you tighten them up," Juli gasps after he's back with us.

"Sometimes you were seen, sometimes you were swallowed by the fog," says Vale.

That gives you courage, I think. But it doesn't help. It's my turn—and once again I have a thick, opaque white wall in front of me.

Juli will later call the line "Gate of the Worlds" because the wall of fog that separates the two sides of Kleines Törl looks like a gate to another world

The opposite side could be 30 or 3,000 feet / 10 or 1,000 meters away; I wouldn't see any difference. But you can feel the length of the line. The vibrations, the mistakes you make while walking, are reflected from the opposite side, and this always takes a few seconds, depending on how long the line is. I think about the foggy highline on the Stawamus Chief two months ago and don't hold out much hope that I'll be able to transmit now.

I balance extremely slowly because the line is so difficult to control without any visual references. My thighs and shoulders are burning. Again and again, I row wildly with my arms when a wave threatens to throw me off. Convulsive, rapid breaths squeeze out of me. I feel reminded of martial arts and keep making indefinable sounds of exertion. My friends can't see me fighting, but they certainly hear my abrupt curses and screams.

And suddenly I hear the others too. That makes me feel better. These are the same voices that cheered me on across the good old Wolfsschlucht five years ago. I no longer felt alone in the white fog. I felt at home.

At some point, I feel that things are looking up again. There are more vibrations behind me than in front of me. The last encouraging calls from Lukas and Juli are much louder than before. The goal must be close.

And am I mistaken, or is there gray rock appearing before me? One more step and I recognize everything. The end of the line, the sling anchor on the rock, my friends crouching up there watching me.

I switch to full concentration so as not to make any mistakes in the final stretch. I continue walking in almost slow motion, and a minute later, exhausted but still slowly and in control, I finally sit down on the line right in front of the rock. Craziness. I crossed Kleines Törl in the air.

And yet, I still don't cry out with joy. Two of our four-person team are successful, but we really didn't imagine it would be this difficult. Two hundred thirty feet / seventy meters should be easy for us by now and pure pleasure! No, it would only be a real success if no one on our team had to go home disappointed.

Thankfully, the fog is clearing more and more, and when Lukas returns from his equally successful walk, the sky is almost blue, and we are bathing in sunshine.

Last up is Vale. We owe him countless divine photos and film recordings, but we must not forget that he is also a strong highliner from the very beginning.

As he too takes the last cautious steps of his ascent, we finally burst into cheers together. Everyone made it! What a team. What a project. It unites different sports and passions as well as the four of us individuals.

* * *

We were in a great mood on the descent. Everyone was proud of themselves and happy for each other. And in the Wilder Kaiser I realized: All the training in the US had paid off. I had returned home and was able to keep up with Juli and Lukas, the pros, my two slackline heroes! That gave my ego a tremendous boost.

The State Examination: Perhaps the Greatest Challenge of My Life (So Far)

MUNICH, BAVARIA, GERMANY
2017

The first few weeks back in Munich after a long slackline trip were always tough. I sat in the lecture hall with a glazed-over look, my heart still far away. In the summer of 2017, I could hardly wait to finally finish my teacher training course and concentrate 100 percent on slacklining for at least a year or two. But there was still one hurdle ahead of me, a gigantic hurdle, bigger than all the ones I had to overcome up to that point: the state examination. To be precise: the first state examination for secondary school teaching in the subjects of English and mathematics.

I spent about a week preparing for the English exams and half a year preparing for mathematics. For the last three months, I'd practically been living in the library, trying to cram in the knowledge I needed from 7 a.m. to 11 p.m. to somehow pass. I found math infinitely more difficult than English. Higher algebra and analysis galore. Groups, rings, bodies—these were all terms I knew all too well from slacklining. What the hell were they suddenly doing in math? It was all so abstract and intangible, so emotionless. I racked my brains and was terrified of failing the exam. I would have had another try, a year later, but I wanted to be free by then! Moreover, if this second attempt also failed, then six years of study would have been for nothing. That couldn't happen. Slacklife was the dream, my *mainline* on which I walked, but teacher training was my *backup*, my security, which gave me the peace of mind I needed to face the future without fear. So I didn't give up.

In the months leading up to the exam, I remembered my experiences at Hunlen Falls again and again, repeating my inner mantra: "If you can walk a free solo world record, then you can damn well pass this state examination. Just don't give up, even if it hurts."

To bring this unpleasant topic to an end: It worked. I passed the exams, and I don't know if I would have really been able to do math if I hadn't learned in the years before on the slackline how to fight, how to push myself to the limit.

Back to the States

CASTLETON, UTAH, USA
EARLY NOVEMBER 2017

We were in the living room of the infamous "Sketchy Andy Lewis" in Moab, a city of 5,000 people in eastern Utah, a true magnet for climbers and other outdoor enthusiasts. The walls were hung with ropes, climbing equipment, and BASE jumping parachutes, interspersed with skull drawings and pictures of scantily clad women. Even a few demonstrative bullet holes from exercises with the "obligatory handgun that every good American household should have, for self-defense," as Ari always tried to convince me. The ground was a sea of miles of slackline webbing. In the middle of it all, Andy and Spencer were sitting, completely stoned, planning the construction of the famous "Castleton" highline. A 1,608-foot / 490-meter stretch between two 330-foot-high / 100-meter-high, freestanding rock towers, at the time the longest slackline in North America.

Andy was rather cautious and skeptical; Spencer was loud in a "It's gonna fuckin' go, let's just do it" tone. It's always wonderful to see the two alpha guys together. Meanwhile, Mia and I taped and sorted the highline setup into three haul bags.

The next morning, we got up at 5 a.m. and set off. In a near-accident on the country road, Andy's hood popped open, so he drove the rest of the way looking out the side window, giving the climbing nerds in the parking lot an original Sketchy impression.

Mia, Spencer, and I carried 150 pounds / 50 kilos of webbing in three attached backpacks 1,310 feet / 400 meters up a disgusting scree path. When we arrived at the top, the Czech crew, consisting of Danny and Peto, who were also on a slackline trip through the US and had spontaneously joined forces with us, had almost reached the Castleton Tower. The other rope team, Catrina from the US and Brent from Canada (Hunlen Falls), were still in the first pitch on the counterpart: the Rectory.

After a lot of scrambling and laying out the webbing in the brittle terrain between the towers, we were finally able to climb up the climbers' fixed ropes. Once we reached the top, we pulled the line up using another rope. Peto and Danny did the same on the other side. Then Spencer, Mia, and I pulled the line tight.

While the sun was already setting on the orange-brown horizon, I started my first attempt of the day, even though I was already completely exhausted and didn't expect to get very far.

Surprisingly, I had control over the 1,608-foot / 490-meter nylon line, a good "don't give a shit" mindset, and was able to speedwalk to the middle. From there it became increasingly difficult. The backup on the other side was completely tight, which made the line swing much more. Plus, Levi's drone was distracting me, and my arms were heavy as lead from a whole day of climbing and rigging.

I remembered something Joel Pinnock had said to me three years earlier at Smith Rock: "You gotta fight without desire."

I said to myself, "Screw it. It doesn't matter if you fall right away. Sending a line is just an arbitrary concept. Let it go."

So I took the pressure off myself and continued to take one shaky step after another. When, contrary to expectations, I finally got to the other side half an hour later and still hadn't fallen, I could hardly believe it. I jumped over the edge with the last step and thus set foot on the Castleton Tower for the first time without having climbed it. But my cry of joy wasn't very loud because I collapsed from exhaustion and let myself fall onto the rock.

> f **November 12, 2017**
> CASTLETON. The longest highline in the United States with ~490m [~1,610 ft] and now my longest onsight walk. It was a freaking hard mission to get up there, rig and tension 500m [1,640 ft] of nylon, but with the endless power and stoke of the French-Czech-Ameri-Ger-Nadian team we got it all done in a day. Just before sunset, I had time for a first crossing and even though my body was tired, the mindset was right, my friends cheered me on, and I managed to walk the whole line on the first attempt.

* * *

However, I can't stay lying down for long because it's slowly getting dark. My friends on the other side have already started the descent and, correctly assuming that I won't want or be able to walk back down the line, have even taken my shoes with them.

Thus begins the scariest rappel of my life. I only have one screwgate carabiner and my HangOver without a screwgate. I clip the first one with a Munter hitch to the fixed rope that the Czechs installed on this tower. I begin to slowly rappel down the 330-foot-high / 100-meter-high wall barefoot and as energy-efficiently yet quickly as possible because my hands are almost unable to grip anymore.

Then a horror situation awaits me in the middle of the wall: Instead of a single rope leading to the next belay station, as I had been previously informed, two ropes are knotted together with a double fisherman knot three feet / one meter below me in the middle of a slippery, vertical slab. It is impossible to pass this spot with the Munter hitch. The rope runs around my carabiner once and clips itself off. A knot wouldn't get past as long as someone is hanging on the rope! Furthermore, this rappelling technique is based solely on friction so I would have to constantly hold the rope beneath me; otherwise I would slip through.

There is no ledge beneath me, nothing on which I could stand or at least support myself with my other hand or elbow. But above me there is another rope team that probably wants to reach the top before nightfall. The half rope dangling three feet / one meter next to me is just within reach and could potentially save my life.

I shout something to them in English and try to explain to them as briefly and concisely as possible my admittedly really stupid and dangerous situation. Thank God they are currently at the belay station about thirty feet / ten meters above me. They secure themselves and secure the rope that hangs down to me. I somehow manage to tie an overhand knot in her rope with one free hand and hang on to it with my HangOver, the one *without* the screw cap.

The climbers' rope stretches, I slide down another three feet / one meter, and only with great pain in my fingers do I somehow manage to free my Munter hitch from the upper strand of the fixed rope. My forearms are pumped up like never before. My arms and legs are shaking. I won't be able to hold this uncomfortable position for much longer. I also notice how the cold begins to travel up my limbs toward the center of my body. There is no time for fear in this situation; I have to use every second and act.

With trembling fingers, I clip the screw carabiner with a Munter hitch to the strand of the fixed rope below the knot. This horrible lump in the middle of the wall, couldn't it have been anywhere else? I have to press my bare feet against the slippery wall one last time. With my left hand, I hold on to the fixed rope above me to relieve the HangOver with which I am still hanging on the climbers' rope and open it. Finally, I can hang with my full weight on the fixed rope that leads me down from this goddamn rock tower.

When I get to the bottom, I feel a hint of relief at finally having solid ground under my feet again. I ignore the cold in my limbs, the growling of my stomach, and the small traces of blood on my forearms and shins. After crossing the last scree field barefoot at a snail's pace, I finally come across the path where Spencer and the others are waiting for me with my shoes. They congratulate me on my first ascent of the line and ask if I'm okay. I comment with a short "Well, I'm alive." I'm too exhausted to shout out loud or give high fives.

With a pained expression on my face and still slightly shocked by the experience, I hobble after them toward the parking lot. This could have turned out very differently. . . .

* * *

Fruit Bowl

Soon better times came again. After Mia, Spencer, and Danny had also successfully completed the "Castleton" highline, we finished the project just in time for the start of the infamous—with over five hundred visitors—largest highline festival in the world: GGBY, short for "Gobble-gobble, bitches, yeah."

Gobble-gobble is said to be the cry of a turkey, as the highline festival overlaps with Thanksgiving, almost as if honoring tradition. It takes place annually at the Fruit Bowl, a huge sandstone canyon twenty-five miles from Moab. Hardly any place in the world is slacklined as much as this one: You can even see the highlines on Google Maps!

For my first day at the Bowl, Ryan Jenks, whom I had met two years earlier in Yosemite, had prepared a special surprise for me: a rope swing into the 330-foot-deep / 100-meter-deep canyon. I already knew this from Germany: Julian and Julius, the same friends with whom I had my first highline experience, had already come up with the brilliant idea of jumping from a 160-foot-high / 50-meter-high railway bridge at the age of seventeen, tied to two climbing ropes. This is how I first experienced free fall. It took me almost twenty minutes before I finally dared to take the first jump into the depths. Two jumps later it was a double backflip and a gainer. Then, a few weeks later I was the first person to do a triple backflip into the pendulum rope.

Here on the GGBY, a rope twice as long was waiting for me. But that alone would hardly be a surprise. I had only seen this legendary highline site in photos and videos. So how about if Ryan blindfolded me from the parking lot to the Fruit Bowl, tied me into the rope swing, and I spent my first seconds of sight jumping into the legendary highline canyon? A brilliant idea that I could hardly say no to.

Despite Ryan's blindfolded escort, the walk over scree and sand felt much more uneasy than walking blind across a highline. Once I reached the canyon, I put on my harness, had Ryan tie me in, and had Mia and Spencer each check several times to make sure that all the knots, carabiners, and ropes were correctly attached.

"Okay guys, I'm ready," I said, my heart beating faster and faster.

My friends started their countdown in unison: "Five, four, three. . . ." At "two," I pulled off my blindfold as agreed, since a completely blind jump and free fall would have been too dangerous.

"One—Welcome to Moab, Friedi!"

As soon as I blinked and noticed the reddish-brown rocks around me and the abyss in front of me, I walked toward it and jumped off. What followed was a free fall of about three seconds, screams of joy, and a huge pendulum. As I swung back, I could already see the impressive vertical rock faces and the first highlines above me. Not a bad start to a week at the Fruit Bowl!

What followed were many sessions on twenty new highlines, lots of rejuvenation, making new international friends, and the wildest parties I have ever experienced. The American slackliners simply know how to party. Especially in the desert. Thanksgiving feasts on camping tables, acrobatics and fire shows in the sand under the starry sky, and quite a few slack-jersey hippies dancing stark naked around oversized campfires to blaring techno music. Some say I was right in the middle of it.

I also had the honor of watching a wedding on a space network. From close up, standing in an exposure turn on a long highline, I watched Ryan and his wife, Kim, exchange vows on a net 660 feet /

200 meters above the gorge. Spectacular and touching. Maybe a few tears rolled down my face. In any case, I thought, "This marriage is kind of cool. Hopefully, someday I'll find a woman crazy enough to do that with me."

Nothing Happens Without Money

Some people may wonder how I financed all my travels and my studies in Munich. The short answer is: slackline and highline workshops for beginners, live shows and keynote speeches at corporate events. So I balanced over the Danube, between church towers, over the Olympic Stadium, and just last summer (2022) over the Munich Tollwood Festival.

In the Christmas edition of the German television program *Wetten, dass . . . ?* in December 2013, I had my first major television appearance, where I narrowly missed out on the competition title, but laid the foundation for my career as a professional slackliner.

In my twenties, I didn't need much else to live on. During the first half of my studies, I lived in a small, shared apartment, then I spent three years in a tiny student bungalow in the Olympic Village, interrupted by my year in the US. Later, between the big trips, a few weeks in my parents' guest room in Bad Aibling.

I ate as was usual among students: lots of noodles, lots of rice, and lots of vegetables. During the winter semesters, I sometimes even managed to live almost entirely from dumpster diving. The nightly rummaging through supermarket trash cans with my Munich friends began as both a thrill and out of ecological conviction. But it also meant that if you do it regularly and with a plan, you can save a lot of money. Giving up was never difficult for me during those days. In my slackline community, I always felt rich and carefree, even without material luxuries.

Dean Potter once said, "Fame and finance have to be second to the drives for perfection and new extremes or the latter wouldn't be strong enough to happen."

So when someone asks me today how to become a professional slackliner, I usually answer something like this: "Anyone who asks themselves this question at the beginning will probably never become one. You have to love slacklining and not give a shit about anything else. Only in this way will sport naturally become your passion, your happiness, and perhaps someday, with a lot of patience, even your livelihood.

Dream Lines

NORTH AMERICA
2018

I still had a score to settle with the most beautiful place I've ever been to. Three years after vowing to return to Yosemite Valley someday, my slacklining and climbing skills were on a completely different level. Now I would be able to fully exploit the highline potential of this magical place. The perfect partner in crime had long been chosen—Lukas.

In October 2018, we had a lot in common. As full-time slackliners, we were both flexible in terms of time and familiar with each other's rigging and working style through numerous highline activities. And we didn't want to waste any time. When we planned a trip together, it was clear from the start that we would make the most of every day and every place. We were lucky: The young Australian slackline and adventure photographer Aidan Williams was traveling on the American west coast and wanted to accompany us. This would ensure that our trip would be photographed appropriately.

Further support came from the Californian slackline freak par excellence: Ryan Jenks. He was immediately excited: Two European slackline pros in his hood! That would provide plenty of material for his YouTube channel.

What you should know about Ryan is that he is a fanatic when it comes to planning: Everything must be prepared down to the last detail. For him, the construction, the "puzzle solving," as he calls it, is often more enjoyable than the highline itself. You can also see this when you watch one of the over 400 videos on his YouTube channel "Hownot2" (formerly "Hownot2highline"). All scenes in which the self-proclaimed "Rigging Nerd" explains something are shot in front of a wall hung with the most colorful, exquisite, and exotic belay and rappelling devices, as well as slackline webbing clamps. Everything flashes and glitters like jewelry and is probably worth no less overall. "Gear porn," that's what real freaks like him call it.

"I'm not very good at walking highlines," Ryan once said to me, "but I'm quite professional at rigging them. And I love it."

So the team was complete, and our goal was clear—even in our minds' eye: Lost Arrow Spire in Yosemite National Park, the famous freestanding stone column with a height of just over 6,890 feet / 2,100 meters. But we had to earn this icon honestly first.

So my second trip to Fairytale Valley began with the same tough, four-hour climb I had made to Yosemite Falls three and a half years earlier. Also in the group: Lukas, Ryan, his wife Kim, Zollie, and Kyle. Once we got to the top, we immediately set up our tents and went to bed early to have enough energy for the next day.

The next morning our motivation was enormous. Lost Arrow Spire should be properly slacked with not one, not two, but three highlines. Ryan had rigged them all before as a California local but never all at once. Lukas and I were jittery and nervous with anticipation. The legendary Lost Arrow Spire, in front of which I had stood three years earlier during our headlamp hike. The most famous highline spot in the world. And a milestone in free soloing. Fewer than ten people had ever walked here without safety equipment, including Andy Lewis, Mich Kemeter, and Dean Potter. And in my eyes, they already belonged to the Slackline Hall of Fame. However, during their unsecured ascent, almost all of them stayed on the shortest line. But there were also the 100- and 160-foot-long / 30- and 50-meter-long tracks next to them, much higher and more frightening. I dreamed of them long before our trip. . . .

Ryan and Lukas formed the rope team that would climb the Spire. While I was climbing a little further up the other side with another climbing rope, a tagline, and a large backpack full of slackline. I had to stay relatively close to the edge and constantly give out webbing—Kyle held the other end in his hand and would later tie it to a rope that Ryan would throw to him from the spire. Finally, I was just above the wall anchor for the 164-foot / 50-meter line and rappelled down to the bolts. Meanwhile, Zollie and Kim prepared the equipment for the other two lines.

I can't remember all the details of the following hours, but somewhere between rappelling, waiting for the others, and tightening the line, there seemed to be enough time for a little selfie video: It shows me with the (unsecured) phone in one hand and the other hand on the Grigri. With the tagline slightly stretched between my teeth, the camera looks below me into a 1,640-foot-deep / 500-meter-deep, vertical abyss to the floor of Yosemite Valley. That brings joy.

After just a few hours of combined efforts, all three lines were set up and tensioned, and Ryan's call came from the Spire: "Fuck! It's perfect. German efficiency meets American gear porn."

The games could begin. We had fun while Kyle serenaded us with his ukulele from the edge of the cliff. Surfing, bouncing, dancing, static tricks, the usual program on highlines of manageable length. Except that these lines weren't exactly at a manageable height. The two longer ones had about 1,640 feet / 500 meters of air beneath them, the shorter "Classic" only about 330 feet / 100 meteres less. It was another 1,640 feet / 500 meters of altitude to reach the bottom of the valley. Within sight and hearing distance, the iconic Yosemite waterfall rushed into the depths, illustrating to us the dimensions of the place. I was involuntarily reminded of Hunlen Falls in Canada.

I no longer felt any fear of heights on these lines. On the contrary, I loved having the abyss beneath me. I often stood in exposure turn for minutes and looked down into the valley, trying to focus my gaze on different places to perhaps see cars or even people. I played with these visuals, looking alternately into the distance, directly into the depths, and then back at my feet, five feet / one-and-a-half meters below me. The safety ring between my feet. Then the narrow one-inch / two-and-a-half centimeter band. Then nothing. It's always absurd what kind of experiences we humans have. Does a bird appreciate what a privilege it is to be at home in the skies?

It wasn't long before Ryan and Kim were walking naked across the highlines, while Lukas and I took turns trying our first handstands on the fifty-foot / fifteen-meter line. We had big plans. On normal slacklines just above the ground, you could sometimes manage ten seconds, Lukas sometimes even more. But doing a handstand on the most famous highline in the world? That would be another world's first and a truly postcard-worthy image. In the end, it was much more difficult than expected. Height does have an impact on balance, especially when the world is upside down.

In my best attempt, I kept my feet up for maybe two seconds. Enough for a snapshot but not very elegant. I didn't care because I actually had a completely different goal for these lines, and I thought the others already suspected it.

"When there's a death consequence, when you are doing things that if you mess up you die, I like the way it causes my senses to peak."—Dean Potter

I have to admit that even though I had done many 100-, 130-, and 160-foot / 30-, 40-, and 50-meter free solos in the previous months, I felt a little uneasy at the thought of doing the "Classic" Lost Arrow Spire Line without a safety leash. At fifty feet / fifteen meters long, I would have the anchor almost directly behind me when I stood up. It would feel awkward, almost like the old tricklines that were now truly years ago. Could I even catch a line like that if I lost my balance? Also, we anchored this line only on the tower side as usual with bolts. On the wall side, we inserted several cams and chocks into a rock crevice and attached the highline anchor to them. Would they really not give a fraction of an inch?

I tested the line a few more times for safety, checking every point. I bent my knees deeply to get used to the old balancing technique of the short lines again. And most importantly, I jumped into the safety leash to put maximum strain on the entire system. None of the clamping wedges gave way. Everything felt as it should.

"It's just Friedi being Friedi," Ryan commented later on camera as I did what I came there to do. I went to the end, took off the safety device, and immediately sat back on the line.

It started. I took one step at a time, slowly and very carefully, aware of the danger but not too nervous. The right level of alertness and presence was there. Not too much tension and not too little. It was almost a joke. I was already in the middle of the line. Less than twenty steps remained until the end. It's hard to believe that such a short line has achieved so much fame.

When the physical challenge is small, the mental challenge of keeping the ego under control is often even greater. You have to be even more careful not to become careless. That was the case here. So I deliberately walked the last few feet even slower and more carefully and kept an eye on the line the whole time as I took my last step onto the rocks so that I could catch it if necessary.

When I reached the end of the line, I let out a subdued "Yippee" because I was still a long way from my goal. The way back was important because that was where I would perform my ritual: Stand in the middle and look down to the side; I hadn't done that on such a short line in a long time.

So I walked back to the middle and stopped. A little more adrenaline came up. But everything went according to plan again, and when I got over there, where Lukas was sitting on the spire watching me, the cheers were even louder.

"You crazy dog," Lukas grinned at me.

I was in a really good mood. And the timing was just right too because the wind was slowly picking up. I glanced at the next longest 108-foot / 33-meter line, which was already shaking slightly in the gusts of wind, and said to myself, "I'm not going to be able to do that one today."

Quit While You're Ahead

The next day, I got up extra early to beat the wind. After a short yoga session, I rappelled down to the anchor point of the "Classic" line and walked over it to the rock tower, from where I could go to the 108-foot / 33-meter line. What was wrong with me? I've never been in such a hurry to get a free solo done. . . . Something was different about this line. Well, not just anything. It was 1,640 feet / 500 meters high!

The walls went down vertically. Sometimes a cold wind came from below the nearby Yosemite waterfall. And the line was definitely a bit more challenging to walk than yesterday's fifty-foot / fifteen-meter classic. The line was "Skypilot," a nylon flat band, heavier and wobblier than the lightweight tubular band of the shorter line. It was also off-level, meaning it was slightly uphill in one direction.

From one hundred feet / thirty meters onward, lines become interesting. For many, this is where the boundary to longlining begins. Not a problem for me, but of the very few people worldwide who have ever walked free solo, the vast majority have stayed in the 65- to 98-foot / 20- to 30-meter range. I think it was primarily the location that gave me a slightly uneasy feeling. I ignored it. Instead, I reminded myself how confident I was at wrestling. If anything went wrong, if I felt even the slightest bit uncomfortable or changed my mind, I knew that within a split second I would catch the line and sit safely on it.

So I slid three feet a meter away from the wall on the line, shook out my arms as usual, and stood up. And it was . . . shaky. Much shakier than expected. One hundred eight feet / thirty-three meters shouldn't swing that much! I was tense. "Exhale!" Counteracting fear is the top priority. Once the fear of falling takes hold of your body, you balance less well and falling becomes more likely. You must not get caught in this potentially deadly spiral when free soloing. But I knew my abilities. The rational part of my brain prevailed: "Exhale" was the magic word. Feel the line, get to know it, take the first step, as I had done thousands of times before . . .

* * *

It works out. The first step comes. It certainly doesn't look as soft and controlled as it should. But who cares what it looks like, I'm only here for myself! I want to get this line now.

I tremble a little less during the next steps. But a basic nervousness remains. I just can't rush into anything. The end is one hundred feet / 30 meters away from me. Theoretically quick to achieve but every step has to be perfect. I can't remember ever feeling the height so strongly in a solo before. It kicks even more than my very first unprotected ascent.

I'm about halfway through now, and I really need to pull myself together. The stretchy band keeps swinging and immediately gives me back all the mistakes I make. I'm grateful for the endurance training on the many longlines because my shoulders and upper arms are already starting to burn slightly. I haven't been on the line for three minutes yet. It is the tension because of the significance of this moment. In addition, in the last quarter, I get slower with every step. I'm still a little confused about how difficult this solo is for me, but at the same time I'm grateful. This line is "next-level shit." I want to walk it solo precisely because it makes your heart sink. And I have to—no—I want to go through it. I know that my stamina and concentration will not let me down.

Only a few feet remain. My arms are burning more and more, but I can still breathe a sigh of relief because I know that I will now finish the line. When I finally get my hand on the anchor and sit down, I don't scream with joy or allow all the tense concentration and alertness to fall away from me. There is no reason for that. I have to stay in the flow to walk back. I find myself in the middle of a 1,640-foot-high / 500-meter-high rock face, without a harness or rope.

I don't take a long break but just shake out my arms and turn toward the Spire. I know I can walk the line; I just did it once. But I'm now on the higher side, the line in front of me goes down much steeper than one would expect from the normal sag on a one-hundred-foot / thirty-meter line. This means I have to lean back and put significantly more weight on my back foot.

The tower seems incredibly far away to me. It's almost as if the line has gotten longer. I'm realizing more and more that this isn't a normal free solo. It is the superlative. The ultimate mental challenge. I have to smile inside about that. That's exactly how it should be, right? This is what I was looking for.

Even though I'm no less nervous, starting off goes better than on the way there. I can hardly understand it myself: Somehow, I'm looking forward to the fear I'll experience in the coming minutes. Because I know that I am about to have one of the most profound experiences of my life. Something I would never forget.

These thoughts go through my head as I approach the center step by step. Apart from these brief snatches of thought—actually, they weren't even complete thoughts, more like emotions, background moods—my concentration remains entirely on the movements of the line, my posture, and my breathing. I've now reached the middle and am slowing down, preparing myself for what's about to happen: the exposure turn.

I have rarely been so excited about something and so afraid of it at the same time. As I turn my feet to the side and my gaze slowly follows, the height almost overwhelms me. I have 1,640 feet / 500 meters of empty space below me—and over half a mile in front of me to the next wall. Completely exposed and detached. A *real* free solo. "Everything else is fake," goes through my head.

Very few people can imagine what it feels like to stand on a one-inch-wide / two-and-a-half-centimeter-wide webbing with nothing to stop you from falling except your own balance. They describe it with words like *unreal*, *out of this world*, *insane*, *absurd*. None of this applies to me. Rather the opposite is the case. When I stand up there and look down, finally holding my life 100 percent in my own hands, I have only just arrived in reality. It's not this moment but rather everything else that feels fake. The everyday. The society. The routine. Everything seems trivial and meaningless. Insignificant. There is hardly anything that gets under your skin, that you really remember forever, that you can be proud of in old age, and then during your last breath, and perhaps in the afterlife. We constantly watch movies, read books, and tell ourselves stories about heroes, brave people who do something extraordinary. Is it any wonder that you want to be the hero in your own movie?

But I only have these thoughts later. As I stand in full exposure on the highest line I've ever walked without a belay, I think about . . .

nothing. I'm in the flow. Time passes without me noticing because my own time stands still. It is the feeling we seek in extreme sports, perhaps even what everyone seeks in ordinary sports or hobbies. My gaze wanders over the coniferous forests in the distance below me, along the gray, craggy rocks and gigantic vertical walls, past the rushing masses of water of Yosemite Falls, and I suddenly feel more connected to nature, to the world, than ever before. The fear is still there, but I let myself go with it, trusting that it will stay at exactly this electrifying level and not turn into panic. I slowly turn back toward the Spire, exhale loudly, and continue balancing.

In the last few feet, I ask myself again whether I'm crazy. Am I normal? Am I mentally ill? What I'm doing here doesn't make any rational sense. And yet it feels 100 percent right. It's *primal*, one of my favorite words, which is difficult to translate to German. *Ursprünglich* (Originally). *Elementar* (Elementary). Connected to the beginnings of humanity, a time when we fought for survival every day and were truly one with nature.

When I finally take the very last step and my foot feels rock beneath it again, I let out a deep, throaty, triumphant cry. I am flooded with so many emotions that it almost overwhelms me. I am grateful, proud, and relieved. At the same time, it feels as if, by stepping onto solid ground, I have returned to reality, awakened from a dream. Or is it the other way around? Is the time on the line reality and now I'm dreaming again? Am I locked in the Matrix again?

I need to sit down, digest everything, and let the adrenaline slowly subside. Then I notice Lukas sitting in the sun on the other side of the gorge, waving to me and shaking his head with a laugh. He must have been watching me from the very beginning of my return journey. I laugh, shake my head as well, and wave back, shrugging my shoulders as if to say, "Well, there's no point. . . ."

And then, I am sure. This is reality, and so is the moment on the line. And I tell myself that everything is fine the way it is, even if the meaning isn't always clear: "Stop thinking about it so much, be happy about what you've already achieved, and above all, stay alert when your ego threatens to take over." Just as the Roman emperors once had someone sitting next to their throne whose sole task was to remind them again and again of their mortality.

* * *

"Strive for rest, but through balance, not through the cessation of your activity." —Friedrich Schiller

The next few days flew by. We took down the three lines, embarked on a long, hard descent, and, as soon as we reached the bottom and had finished our obligatory Philly cheese steak at the lodge, we skied back up the other side of the valley. We camped somewhere in the woods so that we could be at Taft Point early the next day, the very same vantage point where I had been with Joel almost three and a half years earlier and from which Dean Potter had made the last BASE jump of his life. Here, Ryan wanted to put into action a plan he had made long ago: a new Yosemite record distance. A "1,000-footer"—a 296-meter-long highline that was more than twice as high in the middle as it was long.

It just felt great how well the build-up worked with this team. Ryan skillfully flew over a fishing line with a drone, Lukas and I received it, pulled over the tagline, and, finally, the high-tech highline setup: lightweight, low-stretch Spider Silk MK2 from Balance Community.

We all functioned like perfectly oiled cogs in a single, large machine. This made Ryan's rigger heart beat faster. The line was stretched in no time, and despite general exhaustion, Lukas, Kyle, and I all got our send of this new bridge through the American sky. Yosemite's longest line had been crossed; Ryan and Kim took their photos and videos, and the "Germerican" team celebrated another success around the campfire.

During all this, Lukas and I were already planning the next adventure.

The Most Beautiful Highline of all Time

Yosemite National Park encompasses much more than just the famous Yosemite Valley with its Half Dome, El Capitan, campsites, and luxury hotels. There is also the Cathedral Range in the north, a breathtaking mountain range that is part of the much larger Sierra Nevada. The highest mountain in this range, at 10,911 feet / 3,326 meters, is called Cathedral Peak, and this in turn has a slightly protruding western peak called Eichorn Pinnacle, named after Jules Eichorn, a German-American amateur mountaineer who made the first ascent of the lonely rock needle in 1931.

How do you describe nostalgia? It is something infinitely personal. No matter how hard you try to convey to others in words the feeling that comes over you when you think back to a person, a place, a time, you usually fail. I just want to say this: Cathedral

Peak is one of the most beautiful places I have ever been, and the highline at Eichorn Pinnacle is still my absolute favorite among the more than 700 highlines worldwide that I have walked in my life so far.

From a technical point of view, it is relatively unspectacular. Two hundred thirteen feet / sixty-five meters long, about 160 feet / 50 meters high in the middle with a steep 660- to 980-foot-high / 200- to 300-meter-high drop on one side, which at least makes the line seem higher when you are standing on it. The climbing route up the tower consists of two pitches in the upper quad range, nice but nothing too extraordinary. The setup is also comparatively easy and takes less than two hours once you have climbed the tower with the tagline and the rest of the team is reasonably sure-footed.

No, what makes this highline so phenomenal for me is its surroundings. You can stand on the rock needle or later in the middle of the highline, slowly let your gaze wander 360°—and you see nothing, absolutely nothing, created by human hands, except perhaps the highline itself. No trace of civilization. No houses, no roads, no power or radio masts, not even hiking trails, and certainly no people. And even though the nearest road is only three miles away, it still feels like the wildest place I've ever been, even wilder than Hunlen Falls. It's almost as if we've been transported back to a bygone era, a prehistoric time long before human civilization.

That's why I wish today that we hadn't been in such a hurry to complete the three-mile / five-kilometer hike and had taken a closer look at everything. But we couldn't waste any time if we wanted to climb, rig, and highline on the same day. And with a line of this distance, highlining was far from just walking over it. Two hundred thirteen feet / sixty-five meters was the perfect freestyle length, and Lukas and I wanted to make the most of it. You rarely get the chance to do Yoda rolls, shoulder stands, and other new-age highline tricks in the middle of nowhere, surrounded by nothing but rocks, lakes, and never-ending natural coniferous forests.

Thanks to Grant Thompson, we had beautiful video footage, and thanks to Aidan Williams, we had photos that, even without any post-production, created the impression of a magical paradise. Also with them was Yosemite local Robbee Pitts, who Ryan had introduced us to. During the hike, the man in his late thirties, who used to be in the Army, told us, "I walked my first slackline between two Humvees in Afghanistan."

And I thought to myself, "Wow, US military bases in Afghanistan. There really isn't a place where slacklining doesn't happen."

I was grateful for such a small team, of which only two people were serious about getting on the line. Robbee also made a brief attempt, but most of the time remained for Lukas and me. We took turns every forty-five minutes and thoroughly enjoyed this marvel, which had only been rigged *twice* before us. And of course I couldn't resist getting intimate with the line here either. Free solo.

It was almost comical how simple it was. At 213 feet / 65 meters long, the line is to date my fourth longest unsecured walk out of more than a hundred. And yet, it was worlds easier for me than the route at Lost Arrow Spire a week earlier, which was only half as long. It was significantly lower, but at over 160 feet / 50 meters high, a fall would have been just as fatal. But since it was exactly the length on which we regularly practiced our freestyle tricks, I was perfectly prepared for it. Every step felt 100 percent controlled, no wobbling, no nervousness, no tension. Not even when I took off the leash. I cruise. I became one with the line.

After the way there, I did a victory handstand on the rock needle. I think it was one of the best days of my life. In the middle of nowhere. On the way back I stayed in the middle of the exposure turn longer than I ever had in a free solo before. Over five minutes. I just couldn't take in enough of the scenery. I was enthroned above everything, feeling like the king of the wilderness, the mountains, the solitude, and yet inseparably connected to my surroundings. I believe I can rightly classify this moment today as a spiritual experience. In this place, on this line, I felt something that cannot be described in words. Maybe something divine.

Back to the Desert, November 2018

When we returned from the Valley, October was already over, Lukas had to start his journey home, and Ryan was back to work. My twenty-ninth birthday was just around the corner, and I wanted to spend it, if at all possible, at a new highline location, with as many like-minded slackline hippies in an adventurous mood as possible. And so Aidan, Kyle, with whom I had become great friends by now, and I drove in Kyle's van to the second American highline mecca after Yosemite: Moab, Utah. Just in time for November second, we met none other than the legends Andy Lewis and Spencer Seabrooke.

Spencer greeted me with the words, "Happy Birthday, Sweetie!"

In American English, "Friedi" rhymes with "Sweetie," so Spencer has always called me that. He and Andy didn't hesitate for long, packed me into their van, and off we went to my birthday highline location, a small canyon near Moab. Within a very short time, we had set up a 67-foot / 20-meter and a 114-foot-long / 35-meter-long highline, both about 160 feet / 50 meters high.

Ryan once said in an interview, "When Andy Lewis, Spencer Seabrooke, and Friedi Kühne get together, you know that leashes are gonna get dropped."

To this day, I still have the impression that Americans have more understanding and respect for highlining without safety equipment and bombard you with significantly fewer critical questions and stern or even embarrassed looks than Europeans do. Andy, for whom the spot was a real home game, started straight away with an onsight free solo! Phew, that's one thing that's no longer an option for me. But I don't think he even had a harness with him.

Spencer and I walked both lines a few times with the leash before free soloing the longer one. In fact, the shorter line was too sketchy for us. It lay rather precariously on a kind of A-frame made of a few loosely stacked pieces of dead wood. For Andy, this seemed completely normal, and he trusted what he had rigged. Spencer and I felt the residual risk that the entire anchor could suddenly move unpredictably seemed too great. Kind of interesting. Even within the already very specific free solo mindset, there are still big individual differences. Andy was even more excited when I walked the 114-foot / 35-meter line not only without any safety equipment, but also stark naked.

"That's my boy!!!" he shouted across the canyon. "Yeah Friedi!!! That's a real free solo!" That was right up Andy's alley. *Desert Slacklife.*

After all, it was my birthday. You just have to let off some steam. But actually, the cheering and applause, all the "Woo-hoo" and "Fuck yeah, bro," the alpha-male bragging is not what I'm looking for in free soloing, even if it sometimes boosts my ego. For me it's more about quiet, profound, spiritual experiences, the connection to nature and to my true self. But sometimes you need a little variety. And experiencing other states of consciousness, similar to the highlines in Yosemite, should not be missed on this day either. Only it took place in the evening after highlining and with, let's just say, other tools that are common in the American slackline scene.

The Valley of the Gods

November in Utah flew by, and to report on all of our experiences in detail would go beyond the scope of this book. But I want to at least summarize the greatest adventures.

For example, there was our highline in the Valley of the Gods, a truly picturesque sandstone valley in southeastern Utah with gigantic reddish-brown rock towers and plateaus that look uncannily similar to those in the famous neighboring valley, Monument Valley. At the foot of one of these towers, the Eagle Plume, we set up camp consisting of several vans and Spencer's tried-and-tested party tent, the "Mojo Dojo." One thousand six hundred forty feet / five hundred meters away from us, the second rock tower, Tom-Tom, a good 330 feet / 100 meters high, was waiting lonely and eagerly for us to connect him with his partner. This happened in a very similar way to the Castleton project a year earlier. One climb per tower, four people with backpacks full of slackline in the middle, lots of pulling on ropes and yelling at each other, waiting for each other, cursing, readjusting, and, if all goes well, walking the line for the first time just before sunset. This honor went to Andy, and that was a good thing because the project was his idea. He named the line *"Yee naaldlooshii"* ("The Skinwalker"), after a type of witch from Navajo mythology who can take the form of animals to lure people and manipulate them into evil deeds. Why did he do that? Apparently, the line wasn't rigged 100 percent securely when he started his walk. The backup on the other side wasn't secured yet, but Andy couldn't wait, feeling demonically drawn to the line. Just Sketchy Andy. This made it both his personal and the new US length record, thirty feet / ten meters longer than our "Castleton" line the year before.

We spent the next three days climbing the Eagle Plume tower again and again, walking the line from there, celebrating and feasting in the Mojo Dojo tent in the evenings, and almost getting eaten by a puma. Well, the latter might be a bit of an exaggeration, but early one morning Aidan and I discovered some pretty large paw prints in the sand just a few meters from our camp. A little later, on our way to the perfect location for our morning glory photo session, Aidan saw for a split second a large figure on four legs scurry behind a rock. Exciting. "That would have been quite an international meal for the cougar, eh? Some fresh German and Australian meat," Mia commented on our experience with a grin.

She, Spencer, and I all walked the line on our first try. It seemed much easier to me than "Castleton" a year before. And even more beautiful. It is difficult to find words that do justice to the breathtaking sight of the reddish-brown desert landscape, dotted with the majestic, bizarre rock formations that are responsible for the name

Valley of the Gods. Aidan's photos and Spencer's drone footage at least come close. If someone asks me today about my favorite highlines, this line is definitely in the top five, maybe even in the top three. Another exciting experience was watching Andy and Spencer do their BASE jumps from the Eagle Plume tower. I even gave Spencer a PCA, meaning I held his pilot chute behind him to assist so that the main chute would come out and open as quickly as possible. One of the *safer* BASE jumping variants—at least if you trust each other.

I hadn't yet made any plans to start skydiving, but I was already looking with a touch of envy at my friends who, after highlining, skipped the rappel and descending, simply hopped from the tower and flew elegantly almost to camp. . . . I had no idea what lay ahead of me in this regard.

Although I walked the line almost ten times without falling, I didn't try it blindfolded. On the one hand, the surroundings were too beautiful for that, and on the other hand, the blind highline world record was at 1,387 feet / 422 meters, set by my good French friend Pablo Signoret in China. So this record, which I had long dreamed of, was still out of reach. But not for much longer.

The Longest Highline in North America

One week before the annual GGBY Festival, we wanted to beat our recent North American highline record again. All we had to do was extend the same setup we used at Valley of the Gods to 2,950 feet / 900 meters, drive Andy's Jeep to the bottom of the Fruit Bowl, and pull the ledge up with long ropes on both sides.

Thanks to the many helping hands from festivalgoers who arrived early, everything worked out in one day. And the best part was that my friend Pablo had finally joined us from France. The same Pablo who currently holds the blind highline world record. My little Pablito, the then nineteen-year-old extreme sports god, with whom I got along wonderfully since our first meeting in 2014 and who still inspires me today with unexpected life wisdom. At the age of seventeen, he set a highline world record of one mile / 1,609 meters, making him one of the world's greatest slackline talents. But that November, his attention was already on something completely different: BASE jumping. That's why he came to the desert: to throw himself from rock towers and cliffs, yelling along with Andy and Spencer.

How fascinated I was by this sport! I was often there up close and could empathize with the jumpers' emotions all too well. Who hasn't experienced that feeling when you stand on the edge of a precipice and imagine what it would be like to be able to simply jump down and fly away? To be free like a bird? On what is now North America's longest highline at 2,887 feet / 880 meters, I would soon experience the feeling from even closer proximity than ever before.

After I had completed the first ascent and named the new line "Serotonin Overdose," after my favorite Protonica song at the time, Spencer, Mia, and Pablo followed with their sends. It was hardly anything special anymore. We were all so well trained that we and the slackline community around us didn't really expect anything else. It was still no less fun. And you can always take it up a notch by trying to balance faster, backward, back and forth, with your hands behind your back, blindfolded. . . . But Pablo and I were already hatching a plan for a completely new stunt.

The line was almost 656 feet / 200 meters high in the middle. Pablo had already jumped from the cliff next to it and landed safely in the canyon below. It was only logical for him to do a BASE jump from the highline sooner or later, hanging from his arms in the middle, with one or two seconds of free fall and subsequent parachute opening. Basically as "safe" as a parachute jump from a bridge.

I asked him in the afternoon of the second day, chilling somewhere in the sun while others tried the line, "Bro, do you wanna hang from my arms in the middle of this line, and I drop you?"

"Fuck yes, dude!" His answer came like a shot, with his unmistakable French accent. I expected nothing else.

The next morning we got up early to anticipate the thermal winds that came here sooner or later with the sun. We checked each other's harnesses, including Pablo's BASE rig, strapped GoPros to our helmets, and were ready to take off. Pablo balanced with his leash to about the middle, hung himself on a carabiner, and waited for me. I rolled after him the 1,310 feet / 400 meters with HangOver, which was no small feat of strength. He sat comfortably in his harness and looked at his chosen landing zone among the rocks below him. I greeted him for the second time that day with a friendly "Good morning," but by now, we were both tense and nervous. We knew that things were getting serious now and that we needed to concentrate fully. A BASE jump often sounds easier than it is. You only have a few seconds to throw the pilot chute. And if you don't maintain the perfect body position—a slight arch in the back, shoulders symmetrical, arms and legs stretched out—you run the risk of the main chute opening in a twisted position, making it temporarily uncontrollable. Or worse: the pilot chute connecting line wraps around the body and the main chute comes out of the container too late or *not at all.* I was sure Pablo was thinking about all of these scenarios. And about how he would best respond to it.

"Are you ready, dude?" I asked him.

"Check the flap on my container. Is it open? Are the pins in the right place?"

"Yes, it's looking good. Your GoPro is on. How about mine?"

"Yes."

"Okay, let's do it."

We got into position. It was a strange balancing act, as normally two people never hang out in the middle of a long highline. I lay down like I would for a chest bounce, wrapped one leg around the line, and let the other hang loosely for better balance. I pressed my shoulder against the band and let my head hang down slightly on one side. Absolutely uncomfortable, but stable.

Just two feet / half a meter in front of me, Pablo had meanwhile unclipped himself from the carabiner and was slowly and carefully removing his leg, which was hooked in the back of his knee, from the line. He now depended on nothing but his own hands. For most people it's an enormous mental and physical feat, but Pablo is a machine. Now came the moment we had the greatest respect for. The transition from hanging on the line to hanging on my arms. I extended my right hand to Pablo, directly in front of his. My left arm went around the line on the other side and grabbed my right forearm as tightly as I could to give Pablo maximum stability. I definitely didn't want to let him go too soon—or too late and get swept away by him. Although I had already been secured with the leash he had given me shortly before, if I were to slip down at the wrong moment, it could potentially put him into an unstable free-fall position and send him into a spin.

Time slowed down and all these thoughts swirled through my head in just a few seconds. The adrenaline took effect and increased our performance. Hopefully . . .

"You can do this," I said quietly to Pablo, maybe also a little to myself.

He shifted his weight onto his left arm, released the line with his right hand, and within a split second we had each other's right wrists—and we knew we wouldn't let go prematurely.

Pablo looked me in the eyes and said, "Ok, I'm gonna let go with my other hand."

"OK." Now he was just hanging on my arm, 660 feet / 200 meters above the ground. "Fuck yeah, Pablo, I love you so much," I said, to which he replied, "I love you so much."

It's funny what guys say to each other when they're involved in an adventure together. I gave him one last encouraging laugh and said, "This is happening."

He started his countdown: "Three, two, one, love you."

We both let go.

Pablo rushed into the depths before my eyes, toward a gray-brown, rocky background. Moments later, his hand was on the pilot chute, and he threw it cleanly into the wind. Less than two seconds later, his main chute was open, and our cheers echoed through the canyon.

I try to describe everything exactly as it was and how it felt for us. If you have any doubts, I recommend watching the corresponding YouTube video on my channel, which ends shortly after Pablo landed with his face grinning into the camera and with the words "Holy shit, that was fucking insane!"

"Victory is the same as defeat." —Carl Marrs

Now, I was hanging up there all alone, happy that Pablo had successfully completed another BASE challenge, and thinking about whether I would do it one day too. . . . Dropping from a highline with a parachute on my back. It seemed so simple and so logical. With the right preparation, it's almost within reach.

But now, I had a completely different challenge ahead of me, one that I was both excited about and afraid of. The day was still long, the weather conditions were good, and I was in the middle of a nearly 2,950-foot-long / 900-meter-long highline. I had my buff with me because it had been cold earlier. . . . So I decided to warm up by balancing the line to the end, so that on the way back I could make a serious attempt to dethrone Pablo as the blind highline world record holder.

This attempt almost succeeded. If it weren't for . . . well, what actually happened? Wind? Diversion? A backup loop wrapped around the mainline that I would have slipped on? Not enough tension? Too much tension? Nothing like that. My own lack of stamina, and my brain that had given up? That's more likely. The conditions could hardly have been better. No wind, blue skies, mild morning temperatures, a perfectly turned line from the first crossing with Pablo, a light, high-tech setup with good grip (SlacklifeBC Lion and Moonwalk).

As long as you know how to relax and absorb the constant slow but powerful vibrations, soften your body, keep your arms up at all times, and let them make their micro-movements, it's not that much more difficult to ride long highlines blind than with sight. At least physically. At first you feel disoriented, even though you can only walk in one direction anyway. You take your steps much more slowly because you think you have to see what you are stepping on, but that is an illusion too. Apart from the connection every 330 feet / 100 meters, the band is the same everywhere. The human brain is very flexible. When one sense is lost and, therefore, less information needs to be processed by the brain, more work is immediately freed up for the other senses. You can no longer see anything, but you can feel even more. Both the sense of balance in the inner ear and the body awareness are strengthened. The sense of touch in the feet reacts even more sensitively to the pressure created by the vibrations of the slackline. The real mindfuck is that you never know how far it is to the other end. This can really wear you out, especially on particularly long lines. "Where am I? Is it even worth continuing to fight when I still have hundreds of meters ahead of me? Or maybe I only have a few meters left to go and am in danger of walking into a no-fall zone where a fall would be extremely dangerous? When can I finally sit down?" You are afraid of not managing your energy properly; you might want to know if there are gray storm clouds gathering somewhere, and you desperately long to compare the distance you have already covered with the distance you still have to conquer.

These thoughts, which you constantly have to actively fight when walking blindly, have something judgmental, something manic about them. And that is completely out of place when highlining! Without sight, it's more important than ever to take every step as if it were your first. "Fight without desire. Don't think about the send. Enjoy the unspoiled present moment, without evaluating it." These were sayings that Carl Marrs and Jerry Miszewski had told me and that somehow stuck with me. And if you manage to truly let go, then at times balancing with your eyes blindfolded can even seem easier than with your eyes open. Julian Mittermaier told me back in 2015 or 2016 that when the view disappears, the thoughts become more and more calm. Empty your mind.

Back then, this slackline discipline was still a mystery to me, and now I suddenly found myself on the longest highline ever attempted blind.

After initially finding it difficult to start walking blindly, as always, I eventually got into the line with a bit of fighting and arm rowing and built up a good, steady pace toward the middle. But in the last third I had become incredibly hot. I had opened my down vest while walking and was still sweating like a pig because it was now a warm, late morning. How did I know, despite being blindfolded, that I was about in the last third of the route? The setup consisted of several slackline straps, which we tied together at the sewn end loops with a quick link and soft shackle. I knew the lengths of each piece. Apart from the fact that the webbings feel different per se, you will notice it without eyesight at the latest when you step on one of the connections covered with tape. You have to be very careful and lift the leash ring a little so that it slides over the connection. This moment has caused quite a few slackliners to stumble and cost them their send.

But I didn't have that excuse here either. I heard voices from the anchor in front of me. The pre-festival slacklife camp was fully awake. And I, idiot, kept thinking about the blind highline world record. I was stubborn. My arms were already burning, and I realized that I just wanted to get it over with; I was no longer having fun just balancing. I imagined how far I would have to go to the rock for the walk to count, knowing full well that quite a few people would be watching me take the last steps. I thought of Pablo. Would he resent me if I broke his record now? Of course not, what a stupid thought. He would be proud of me. In general, there were too many thoughts going through my head. Too much extrinsic motivation. Where had the flow of pure balancing gone?

The line became steeper, and the frequency of the oscillations increased. The end was near. I felt stiff and tense, no longer able to smoothly absorb the big waves and let them pass through me. On the contrary, I cursed and screamed every few steps. And worst of all, I was afraid of falling. I kept thinking about falling and how many more steps I would have to take before it would finally be over.

"How far, guys?" I said in agony, in fits and starts, but as loudly as I could, not knowing how far away my friends were from me.

"You got about thirty meters [one hundred feet] left, Friedi. Keep going," the gentle, relaxed voice of the Canadian Danny rang out. It sounded like he was right next to me, the heightened senses of a blind person at work, and yet: Thirty meters? So far? I had hoped the answer would have been five or ten meters, then I would have taken a few more steps and sat down.

"You got this, man," I heard Pablo's familiar voice. So he had already climbed back up after his BASE jump and was now watching me too. "But I don't got this," I thought to myself. I had little control over the webbing anymore. I trembled with every step, and my thoughts were everywhere but where they should be. And I was at the end of my strength.

After someone shouted to me that there were only about thirty feet / ten meters left, "You're almost there, man," I couldn't take another step. I stood in one spot for several minutes, struggling, desperately hoping, praying that the monster beneath me would calm down again. But the opposite was the case. If you are close to the anchor of a long line and do not relax, soften your body, and find your center, then the line will only rock further with every balancing movement of the arms. Until it's over.

The craziest thing was that I didn't even fall into the leash but caught myself on the line! Did that mean: I wasn't at the limit yet? Could I have continued fighting? I don't believe so. I was just done. I screamed various obscene words through the canyon as I fell and immediately heard "Nooo" and "You had it, man" coming from the anchor, as well as a bit of applause and shouts of joy in the distance.

When I took the blindfold off my head, I had to blink hard because of all the light, but that was definitely not the only reason why a few tears soon rolled down my face. I hit my forehead, slapped the webbing in front of me with the palm of my hand, and cursed myself. There were really only thirty feet / ten meters left to the end. I could have skipped the last seven to ten feet / two to three meters before the wall, just to be on the safe side, as was usual on most walks.

Once I had solid ground under my feet again, I was greeted with many encouraging hugs. Quite a few of the slackliners gathered said things like, "Come on, man, it basically counts," "You walked all the way," or "You walked 99 percent. Who cares about the rest?"

There were certainly arguments. Quite a few people in the history of slacklining, among them some of the supposedly best, have counted some lines as walked without actually walking all the way to the end, and in my situation, they might now be celebrating their new world record. I have witnessed it several times, but I have never criticized anyone for it. It's true. What are twenty feet / five meters out of a 300-foot / 100-meter line? What are thirty feet / ten meters out of a 3,000-foot / 1,000-meter line? Everyone should have their own standards, at least when it comes to personal progress. Slacklining was still a relatively young and unregulated sport. No Olympic committee had ever laid down in black and white how a highline should officially be walked.

For a moment, I was tempted to write the line off as a blind send. But only for a tiny moment. I knew I wouldn't be happy with that in the long run. If I had sat down in a controlled manner thirty feet / ten meters from the edge, it would have been different, but I was determined to walk a few more steps and lost control. It wasn't clean. Not by my standards. And I knew it wouldn't have been a crime according to the standards of one of the eyewitnesses and someone very close to me: Pablo. He held the record, and his recognition and friendship were incredibly important to me. When he hugged me without saying a word and I noticed his very neutral, hesitant expression, I knew: He wouldn't contradict me if I now agreed with the "You walked all the way; it basically counts" people. But he might lose a spark of respect for me. This strengthened my decision: Without lows, there can be no highs. Today I had failed, but one day I would break the blind highline world record.

© Diethard Kühne

Cliff diving in the Jenbach Valley: Friedi, aged eleven, with his younger sister, Luise, and his childhood friend, Höfi

The Inntal gang: Valentin Rapp, Julian Mittermaier, Lukas Irmler, and Friedi

© Valentin Rapp

Urban highline world record above the Munich Olympic Stadium in 2015

© Johannes Olszewski

Church tower highline in Ingolstadt with a leash Swami

Friedi on the classic 230-foot / 70-meter highline at the Wendelstein in Upper Bavaria with a two-pint tankard of beer: even the tankard was leashed in for safety!

© Benedict Martin

Friedi is (still) chilling with his safety harness, while next to him the water plunges 1,300 feet / 400 meters.

Pure euphoria after the free solo world record

The Hunlen Falls team (from left to right): Valentin Rapp, Friedi, Matt Davis, Louie Wray, Spencer Seabrooke, Levi Allen, Lukas Irmler, Brent Plumley, Mia Noblet, Michael Neureurer, Sanja Radov

Friedi and Michael's jaws drop when they see the waterfall.

Spencer Seabrooke, aka The Minister of Bacon Affairs

Highlining under the stars at Stawamus Chief in Canada

The Gate of the Worlds in the Wilder Kaiser

Slackliners from all over North America and some from as far away as Europe meet at the annual Squamish highline gathering.

GGBY, the world's largest slackline festival, attracts hundreds of adventurers to Moab, USA, every year, with highlines, rope swings, space nets, and BASE jumps.

Eichhorn Pinnacle, which Friedi calls the "most beautiful highline of all time"

© Aidan Williams

Surfing until your thighs burn, for Friedi the second most awesome feeling of balance—after free solo

Rappelling at a height of over 3,000 feet / 1,000 meters can be so much fun, especially when the reason for it is to rig a highline to the Lost Arrow Spire.

© Ryan Jenks

The Eichhorn Pinnacle team (from left to right): Aidan Williams, Grant Thompson, Friedi, Robbee Pitts, Lukas Irmler

Friends for life: Lukas and Friedi on top of Eichhorn Pinnacle in Yosemite, USA

Friedi treats himself to a deep look into the abyss while balancing free solo in the exposure turn on the classic highline at Lost Arrow Spire.

© Kyle Lovett

Mia Noblet walks a 1,640-foot / 500-meter highline in the Valley of the Gods, while Andy Lewis BASE jumps from the rock tower behind it.

© Aidan Williams

GGBY 2018

© Aidan Williams

When the desert becomes a dance floor

© Aidan Williams

With his LED costume, Friedi becomes an angel floating above the abyss.

© Aidan Williams

© Aidan Williams

Friedi on the final feet to the blindfolded highline world record . . .

© Aidan Williams

. . . but then he falls just before the end.

Long snow hikes to highline in Alaska

© Aidan Williams

Mia and Friedi at Angel Rock

© Aidan Williams

Greetings from the Empire: Friedi on a Star Wars-like gold mining rig rusting away in the middle of wintery Alaska.

© Aidan Williams

Aidan was able to capture a hint of the Northern Lights with this photo of Mia.

© Aidan Williams

© Tanois Nassar

Thanks to the Crossing Lines association, people can now balance across the desert sand in refugee camps in Lebanon.

© Tanois Nassar

Immediately after their wedding, Friedi and Homa went highlining in the Frasdorf Dolomites.

Martin Freitag

© Sergey Shakuto

Moscow 2019: Urban highline world record

As in the West, so in the East: The Russian slackline community runs its small highline festival in Kislovodsk with passion and joy. © Aidan Williams

Blindfolded highline world record 2019 © Aidan Williams

© Aidan Williams

An adventurous road trip from Russia via Georgia and Armenia to Iran begins for Friedi, Sasha, Vova, Jaan, and Aidan.

© Aidan Williams

The police, your friend and helper—and sometimes your fan

Sasha on Georgia's longest highline © Aidan Williams

© Aidan Williams

You have to chill sometimes—especially if, like Sasha, you drive a big van full of slackliners through the countryside all day.

Friedi hovers over the old mining town of Chiatura. © Aidan Williams

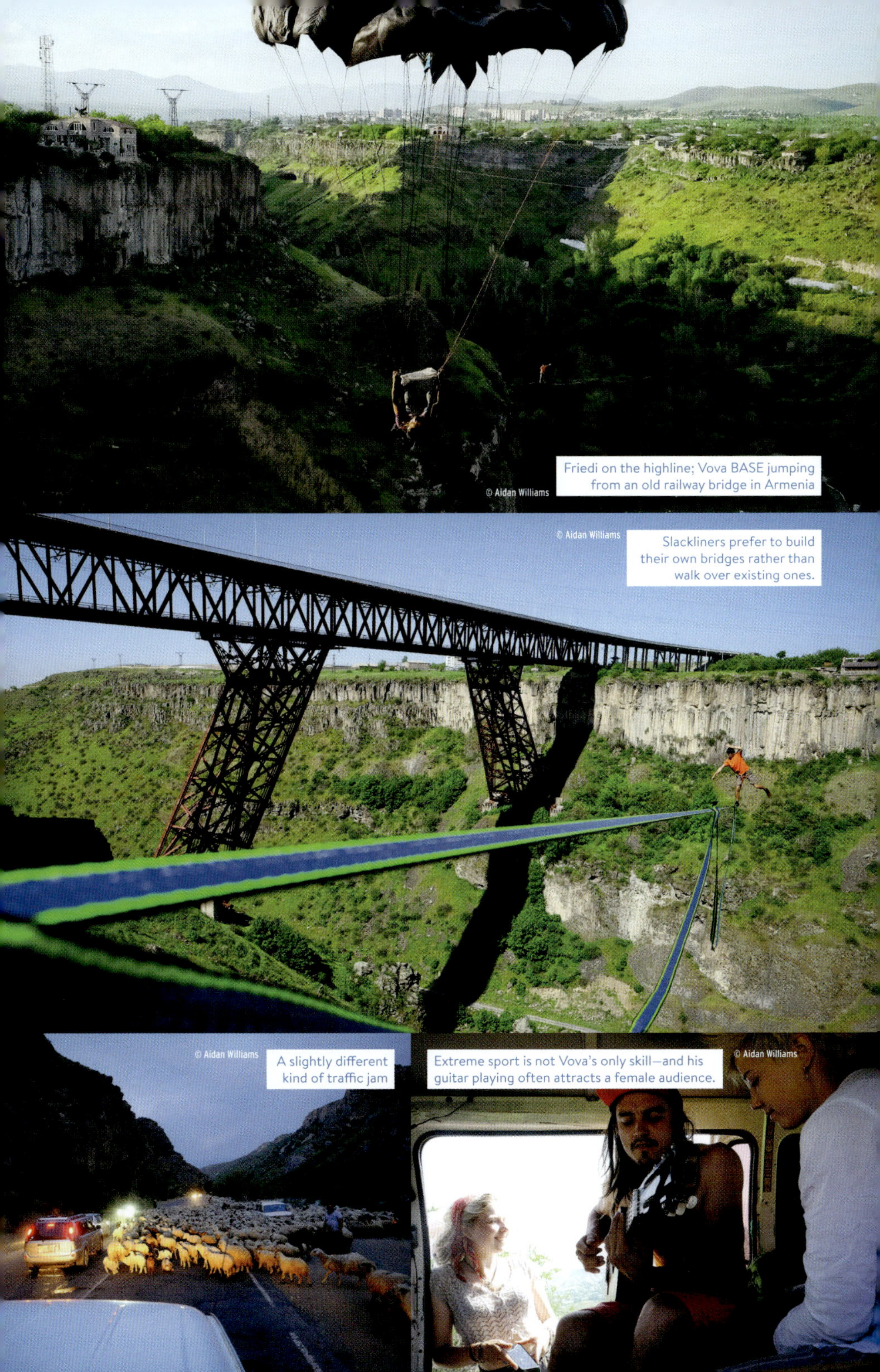

Friedi on the highline; Vova BASE jumping from an old railway bridge in Armenia

© Aidan Williams

Slackliners prefer to build their own bridges rather than walk over existing ones.

© Aidan Williams

A slightly different kind of traffic jam

© Aidan Williams

Extreme sport is not Vova's only skill—and his guitar playing often attracts a female audience.

© Aidan Williams

A brand-new power pole, without cables or electrical connection yet, that you have to drive a long way through rural Armenia to find

© Aidan Williams

The construction, the "rigging," is an art, a craft, and an ever-changing puzzle.

© Aidan Williams

From left to right: Vladimir (Vova), Friedi, Sasha, and the Armenian car mechanic who repaired our Toyota

© Aidan Williams

Probably the world's first and only highline ever rigged between two power poles

© Aidan Williams

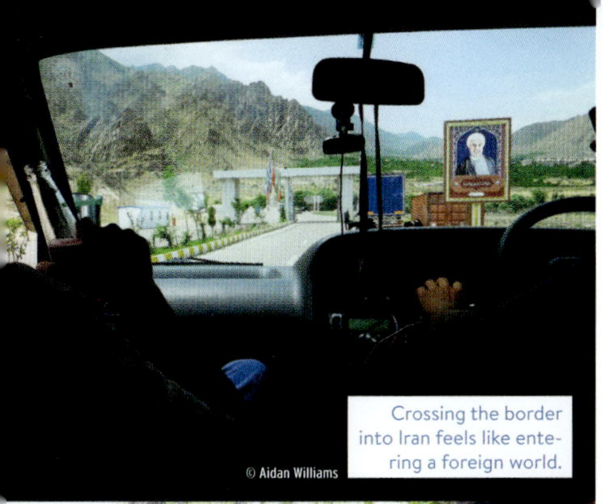

Crossing the border into Iran feels like entering a foreign world.

© Aidan Williams

The Persian slackline community shows what true hospitality is.

© Aidan Williams

© Aidan Williams

Night highline session high above Tehran, a city with over eight million inhabitants

© Aidan Williams

Anya Vlasova from Russia also made it to Iran to meet up with the community and Friedi's friends for highlining.

© Aidan Williams

Above: Vova from Russia
Below: Siavash from Iran

Jaan during the first ascent of the last highline that Friedi's friends made in Iran © Aidan Williams

Slacklining connects people. © Aidan Williams

With the right atmosphere, even a meal around the campfire becomes a feast. © Aidan Williams

Free solo at sunset in the mountains in Golestan, Iran © Aidan Williams

Selfie on the highline: After the wind-related failure so close to the world record, Friedi is initially devastated.

When Friedi began crossing the world's longest slackline, the weather was still good.

© Aidan Williams

But two hours later, he arrived on the other side in storm and rain.

© Flowish Motion

Mia Noblet walks the "shorter" 0.6-mile / 1-kilometer line in Norway and sets the female highline world record.

The 0.6-mile / 1-kilometer line becomes a gigantic sail in strong winds.

© Kfir Amir

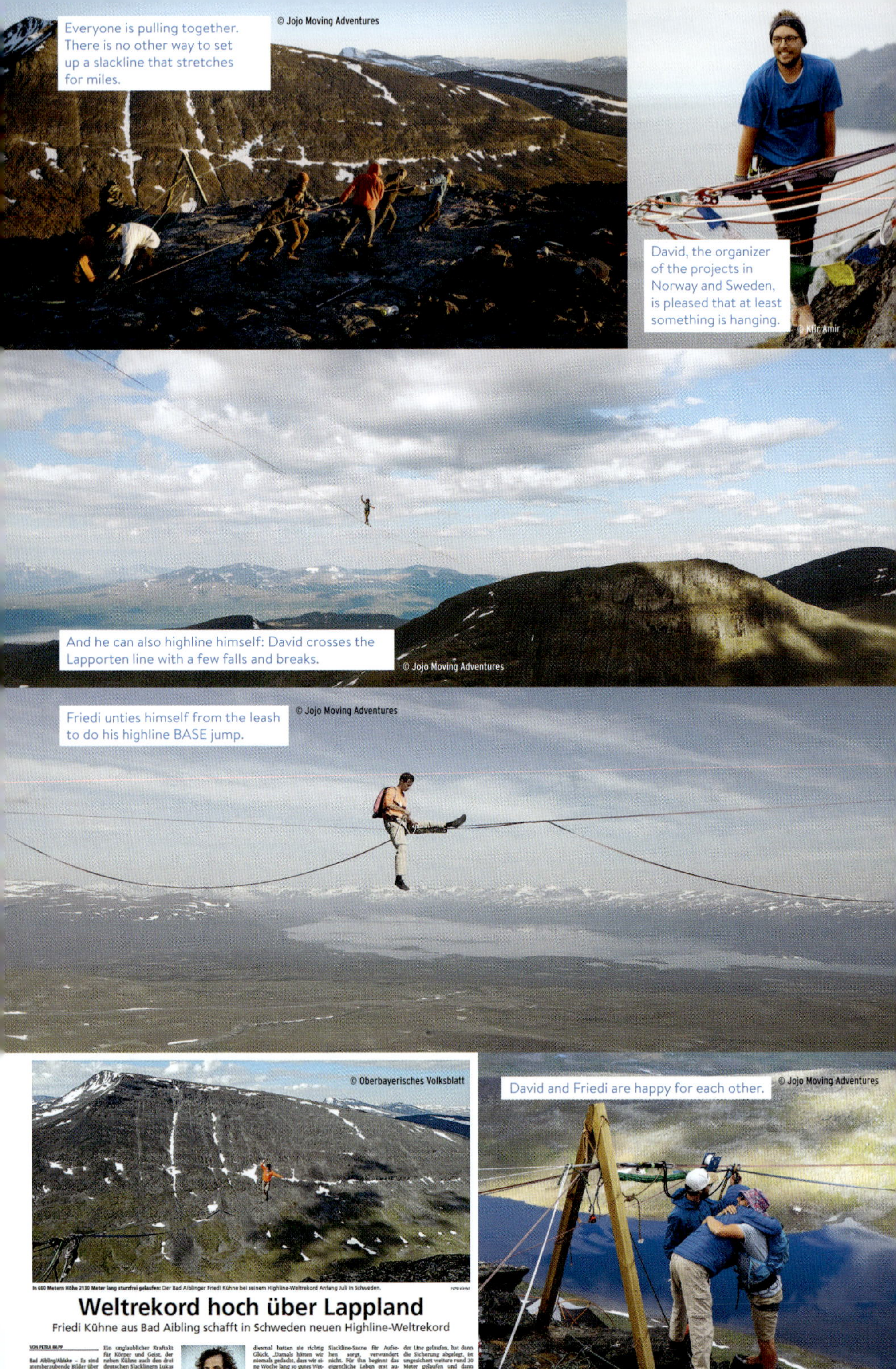

Everyone is pulling together. There is no other way to set up a slackline that stretches for miles.

© Jojo Moving Adventures

David, the organizer of the projects in Norway and Sweden, is pleased that at least something is hanging.

© Kfir Amir

And he can also highline himself: David crosses the Lapporten line with a few falls and breaks.

© Jojo Moving Adventures

Friedi unties himself from the leash to do his highline BASE jump.

© Jojo Moving Adventures

© Oberbayerisches Volksblatt

In 600 Metern Höhe 2130 Meter lang sturzfrei gelaufen: Der Bad Aiblinger Friedi Kühne bei seinem Highline-Weltrekord Anfang Juli in Schweden.

Weltrekord hoch über Lappland

Friedi Kühne aus Bad Aibling schafft in Schweden neuen Highline-Weltrekord

VON PETRA RAPP

Bad Aibling/Abisko – Es sind atemberaubende Bilder über einer atemberaubenden Landschaft: Hoch über dem Lapporten-Tal in Nordschweden in der Nähe von Abisko

Ein unglaublicher Kraftakt für Körper und Geist, der neben Kühne auch den drei deutschen Slacklinern Lukas Irmler aus Miesbach, Quirin Herterich aus Altenau und Ruben Langer aus Sachsen dort gelungen ist.

diesmal hatten sie richtig Glück. „Damals hätten wir niemals gedacht, dass wir eine Woche lang so gutes Wetter haben würden, und der hochkomplexe Aufbau so gut klappen würde. Und dass dann noch vier Leute

Slackline-Szene für Aufsehen sorgt, verwundert nicht. Für ihn beginnt das eigentliche Leben erst außerhalb der Komfortzone, und Angst ist nicht sein Ding, schreibt der Extremsportler, der jetzt auch das

der Line gelaufen, hat dann die Sicherung abgelegt, ist ungesichert weitere rund 30 Meter gelaufen und dann gesprungen: „Ich habe mich dann in exposure (Blick zur Seite) gestellt und mich runterfallen lassen. Bei dieser

David and Friedi are happy for each other.

© Jojo Moving Adventures

December 3, 2018

"Victory is the same as defeat."

About 870 [2,850] out of 880 m [2,880 ft]. The blindfolded highline world record was right there within my reach. And then I fell. I had a bunch of fights earlier during the walk and was sweating and screaming toward the end. My friends at the anchor shouted at me how much distance I had left, and I wanted it so bad. But then, the last fight was just too much, just when the big highline softness disappears and it gets shaky like a longline. I caught the line, took the blindfold off, and saw how far I had gone and how little was left. It reminded me of when I sent nearly 1600 m [5,250 ft] in 2017, and I was equally frustrated. But these moments are where we can truly grow and snatch a psychological victory from a technical defeat. Some suggested that I could consider this a send, having walked more than 95 percent of the line without falling. But I didn't end my walk in a controlled way. I value the sport and the records too much. So this one remains with you for now, Pablo Signoret. Let's try again before too long.

Alaska

FAIRBANKS, ALASKA, USA
DECEMBER 2018

Why? Why travel to Alaska, the northernmost state in the US, in winter? Wouldn't there be a better time for this? "No," Aidan thought. Because he had something very special planned.

Everyone has seen a picture of the mystical green glowing sky, caused by the collision of electrically charged particles of the solar wind with oxygen and nitrogen atoms in the Earth's upper atmosphere. How crazy would it be to balance under this magical sky fire and take a photo of it? Aidan was ready to give everything for that one shot.

Finding the right slackliners for the project was the least of his challenges. Mia and I were immediately excited about his idea of flying from Salt Lake City to Fairbanks at the end of November. Alaska. Winter. The three. That sounded like coldness, silence, even thoughtfulness and introspection. And I think that's exactly what we were in the mood for after a month in the hot Utah desert, with one highline project after another, hundreds of people, and some admittedly extravagant parties.

On the flight to Fairbanks, I recalled what I knew about Alaska. There wasn't really a slackline community there. We would have to find accommodation and highline spots ourselves somehow.

I thought of the story of Christopher McCandless, aka Alexander Supertramp. The adventures of the twenty-two-year-old American, who decided to leave bourgeois society behind, were first written down in the book *Into the Wild* by Jon Krakauer and later made into a film under the same name. The story ends in Alaska, where the young runaway spends a summer living in the wilderness, experiencing true freedom and finding himself.

But the story doesn't have a happy ending. The last pages of Alex's diary testify to how much he misses his family and how empty the great experiences feel when there is no one to share them with. I think I can relate to many of Alex Supertramp's experiences today.

Friday, 11/30/2018

After the first night in the basement belonging to our Couchsurfing host Seth, we set off in the rental car to the first highline. Stop at Safeway: Outside in the parking lot, it's 14°F [-10°C], and there are huge piles of snow; inside it's comfortably warm, and on the shelves cooled down with electricity, there are pineapples, mangos, avocados, even damn watermelons.
Crazy....
Then we rig a cute, 15-meter-long [50-foot-long], about 30-meter-high [100-foot-high] highline over a small gorge. After my obligatory, probably first and only free solo ascent in all of Alaska,

it is already dark. Thick fog blocks our view of possible Northern Lights. Shit. What follows is the coldest night I have ever spent in a tent. According to Aidan's thermometer, it's -4°F [-20°C]. But the three of us in a two-man tent with thick down jackets and sleeping bags barely feel cold and eventually even fall asleep.

At five in the morning, Aidan's gentle voice with an Australian accent: "Guys, the fog has almost lifted. Let's see if we can get a shot." I look out and think to myself, "No way. You can't see anything at all." Mia finds it easier to get up and she grants Aidan his wish.

Indeed: Back in the tent, Aidan presents us with a photo of Mia, in which a very subtle, faint, green glow can be seen in the background. Not really *the* shot, but maybe a taste. There's more to it. But not that night. The clouds have become thicker again, so it's time to take everything down in the light of our headlamps and head home.

We made our second attempt at a line suitable for photographing the Northern Lights at Angel Rock, an imposing rocky peak about fifty miles east of Fairbanks. It towers several hundred meters above the surrounding, never-ending green coniferous forests and therefore attracts countless hiking tourists in the summer. And in winter absolutely no one. Except us.

There was no climbing topo for this area. Apart from a glance at the map, we had no idea what to expect there.

Once we arrived at the rock, the scenario quickly became clear. On the opposite slope, a large boulder could be easily wrapped around, and the slackline could be carried from there to the foot of the approximately 130-foot-high / 40-meter-high rock. But how should we get on this one? Somehow, we had assumed that there was a normal route there: a route with a maximum difficulty level of second to third, which we would be confident enough to tackle even in winter without any safety equipment. There was something like that too, but the walls were damn steep and slippery.

All three of us cautiously moved to a slightly higher ledge so that we could scout out a potential route with as many eyes as possible. Then we pushed and pulled each other up to a second ledge. There was significantly less space for the three of us. We could guess what was going to happen next, but it was impossible to predict whether we would be able to get to the top on this route in the winter conditions—and whether we would be able to turn back if necessary. We had a one-hundred-foot-long / thirty-foot-long rope with us, but nothing to tie it to. No wedges or cams. There was no trace of bolts on this wall.

"It's kinda sketchy, don't you think?" said Mia.

"Yeah, let's not force it," joined Aidan. "If it doesn't go, it doesn't go. We'll find a different line."

But I thought there was a good chance I could make it up there, and I was sure that once I was at the top, I would have no problem placing some bolts for a super-cool new highline, which I could then use to rappel elegantly. Because one thing was certain: climbing down was unthinkable with so much snow and ice on all the holds and footholds. It could go up.

So I set off with a drill, bolts, and rope in a small backpack. I was climbing at a snail's pace. I brushed every ledge, no matter how small, free of snow with my gloves before climbing onto it. Unfortunately, the terrain up above didn't get any easier. A few times I took off a glove to put my hand into a crack, after which I had to take a break for minutes each time to warm my hands up for the next hold.

I was now about thirty feet / ten meters above my friends. A sudden climb back onto a ledge just below me was usually still possible, but a real slide or a stagger backward would have ended in disaster. Next to the ledge where Mia and Aidan were standing, the drop continued for another 160 feet / 50 meters. What the hell was I doing here again? I was no longer sure whether I would be able to climb back down to my friends in a controlled manner. I had to go up, but I never knew exactly what awaited me after the next one-and-a-half feet / half meter of slow-motion climbing. Was a highline really worth it? Each move was still clearly within my comfort zone, but the amount of snow, the ice, and the uncertainty made it, from my current perspective, the stupidest free solo I have ever climbed.

I was now so high that the summit couldn't be all that far away. The next ledge was just above my head, but there were no good footholds on the steep wall below, just dangerously inclined, slippery slopers that I didn't dare stand on. The thought of not being able to go any further now sent a chill down my spine. I haven't been able to see my two friends for a long time. Then, I spotted a small purple loop, almost two feet / half a meter above me, half frozen. Aha! So people had already climbed up here before me. It's crystal clear. But probably at a completely different time of year. The loop was placed around an hourglass and knotted, so it was supposed to hold me. But she was not yet within reach. OK. Now full concentration and determination. Waiting too long doesn't help. I started brushing the sloper free of snow, at the height of my knees, as if my life depended on it. Well, maybe my life would depend on it. Then I did the same with my shoes, trying to dry them as much as possible, and then pressing my left foot onto the small, inclined plate at the ideal angle with maximum contact surface. I slowly shifted my weight forward, simultaneously standing on tiptoe with my right foot and pushing my upper body tiny bit by tiny bit along the wall in front of me. It was a balancing act. I stretched further and further up. I had probably never been as big in my life as I was at that moment. If the situation hadn't been so serious, I would have thought back to my childhood basketball dreams.

My weight was now almost entirely on my left foot, and it was only standing on friction because the step was so steeply inclined. The small purple loop was less than an inch away from my right hand, but I had reached my limit in terms of body length. Okay, concentrate even more. "There's no way you can miss this sling," I said under my icy breath. Yes, I often spoke English to myself on these trips. This was followed by a hop of about two inches. Not a real jump at all, more of a tiny, dynamic upward jump, with my right foot leaving the safe ground beneath me. It felt like the biggest dyno in my entire climbing history. My right hand had grasped the loop with precision, my left hand immediately followed, and I was now able to pull myself onto the next ledge. To my immense delight, it was the last one. In front of me lay a flat peak, a few dozen square feet wide.

I laughed out loud with relief. “Guys, I made it! I’m at the top!” I called to Mia and Aidan. And they were certainly as relieved as I was.

After a bit of exploring, I found a really nicely set up rappel anchor with two well-preserved bolts. Another of our removable bolts and that would make a magnificent highline anchor. After drilling, I threw the rope down the steep wall in the direction of the planned highline, waited until my friends had secured everything, and pulled up the 230-feet-long / 70-meter-long line and the remaining anchor material in one go. While Mia finished stretching the line on her side, I was already in such a good mood and relaxed that I treated myself to a little victory handstand in the middle of the summit plateau before the first ascent of Alaska’s longest highline.

The rest of the day flew by. I walked the line, Mia walked the line, we filmed some tricks, Aidan dug through snow and bushes to get the coolest photo angles, and I landed what was probably the world’s first Yoda roll in 14°F. But the sky didn’t clear up that day either, so we had to return home once again without a photo of the Northern Lights.

Tuesday, 12/4/2018

A little bit of tourism.

The small town of North Pole is not actually located at the North Pole but is decorated with Christmas decorations all year round. Once there, we are spotted by the mayor himself as we are about to accidentally park in the snow-covered staff parking lot of the town hall. Small, round, and bearded, the gentleman himself could almost pass for Santa Claus. When he hears that a German, an Australian, and a Canadian have come to Alaska to go slacklining in the winter, he enthusiastically invites us to his office for a hot chocolate to hear our story.

But it ends with *him* telling *us* his story in great detail. Mr. Mayor was stationed in Frankfurt at some point, speaks a few words of German, was given the office of mayor as a reward for his many years of service in the Army, and so on. Mia, Aidan, and I secretly exchange bored glances.

When we leave his office two hours later, we are warm, but we don't have enough time to scout highlines. Instead, another item on the unwritten Alaska list is checked off: a winter water iceline.

On the outskirts of North Pole, we stretch a 40-meter-long [13-foot-long] slackline over a river next to a bridge. It is not completely frozen due to its high flow speed, but the edges are covered with ice about five meters [16 feet] wide. Mia and I both balance barefoot, but with all our clothes on. Falling in is not an option. A quasi-free solo.

All Good Things Come in Threes

According to the weather forecast, we only had one last night left for a potential Northern Lights highline. Again, the tip came from our brilliant Couchsurfing host, Seth. He told us about the Chatanika Gold Dredge, a large, almost 100-year-old gold mining facility that stood in the shallow waters of the river of the same name and had been rusting away since 1958. A relic from the time of the great gold rush in Alaska and less than thirty miles from Fairbanks. Highline or not, we just had to see it.

My first thought when we stood in front of the huge river dredger was *Star Wars.* It was like a crash-landed spaceship or an AT-AT Walker that had fallen over on the snow planet Hoth from *Episode V: The Empire Strikes Back.*

It was bitterly cold by now, but that didn't stop us from exploring the river dredger extensively and climbing around on it. I was reminded of my childhood when I explored the abandoned Kolbermoor spinning mill with my friends. It was exciting back then: scrambling around between 100-year-old factory equipment, through corridors, shafts, and huge empty halls, over drafty stairs and fire escapes, exposed to the ever-present danger of stepping on broken glass or pigeon droppings—or getting caught. This childlike urge to explore was still there when I was twenty-eight. And Mia felt exactly the same way.

Soon, we met again on top of the Gold Dredge, like in the crow's nest of a sailing ship, and took a selfie. Aidan took it a bit easier with the climbing, apparently making plans for the best photo angles. There were so many steel cables crisscrossing the mining facility, that you were almost tempted to forgo the highline and just balance on one of them. But that seemed too sketchy to us.

So we rigged our last highline in Alaska from one end of the gold-mining facility to the other, about fifty feet / fifteen meters above its deck. We each walked once in daylight and then went back to the car to wait out the night in the warmth. And this one was . . . cloudy again. This sucks. On top of that, the clouds didn't seem to have the slightest influence on the night's cold. Aidan's thermometer showed -11°F /-24°C. *Negative eleven degrees Fahrenheit!* This was by far the coldest highline activity I have ever been involved in. That alone made the line worth walking at night.

So we headed to the river at midnight. Aidan got into position on the hill next to it and Mia and I climbed the rusty ladder up to the small platform from which our highline started. We both wanted to go there and back once, but that was definitely not what we could do. I let Mia go first, which meant that my feet got so incredibly cold while I waited that I decided to put some of the heat packs I had stuffed in all my pockets under the soles of my feet in my Sole Runner shoes. Sure, extra-thin soles are great for slacklining, but they hardly insulate. And even the wool socks that my mother had knitted with so much love were no longer of any help. A chemical heat reaction was needed.

However, this made balancing much more difficult. With great difficulty, I managed to walk the approximately 150-foot-long / 45-meter-long line. At night, with barely any light and -11°F /-24°C. Wow. I stopped in the middle and looked sideways at Aidan, who gave me a quick thumbs up and then alternated between fiddling with his camera and putting his shaking hands into his jacket pocket, which was definitely filled to the brim with heat packs.

On the way back, I saw Mia, also with her hands in her jacket pockets, hopping from one foot to the other, and with a smile on her face. This was a slackline adventure just to her taste. At the limit. Above me, the cloudy night sky had opened up a little and although I didn't see any northern lights, I did see a few twinkling stars. Meanwhile, Aidan took some of my absolute favorite slackline photos. Me floating above the stranded *Star Wars* spaceship, in a winter wonderland under the starry sky. A picture like from an alien planet that almost makes you shiver with cold just by looking at it.

This last night and this last highline were a worthy end to our Alaska trip, even without the Aurora Borealis.

And now we have been freezing long enough...

THE EAST

Tuesday, 7/16/2019

Bekaa Valley, Lebanon

Two slacklines stretched with ground anchors and A-frames in the middle of gravel and desert sand. That's all it takes to create perhaps the happiest and most grateful faces I've ever seen. My slackline buddy, Tanios Nassar from Beirut, took me to a Syrian refugee camp. There, as part of the international, non-profit organization Crossing Lines, he offers slacklining once a week for children who had to leave everything they love behind during the war.

The approximately thirty boys and girls wait patiently in two rows in front of the slacklines. They can hardly wait for us to lead them by the hand across the wobbly belt, stretched over the rugged desert sand that has become their new playground. Some of the boys are quite rascals, pushing each other, and a fight breaks out. Tanios intervenes and says something in Arabic that calms them down. I look into innocently grinning faces, surrounded by black, messy hair. Deep brown eyes, which have seen more than one should at this age, return my gaze with curiosity and hope. When, after a full hour of practice in the sweltering heat, the first children balance a

```
few steps on their own and the feeling of success
is reflected in their beaming little faces, I
have to hold back tears.
We actually came here to give something to the
children, but after this experience I feel richer
than ever.
```

Which Trips Should You Write About?

A look at a world map reveals that there is significantly more landmass to the east of Germany than to the west, with four times as many people. Not to mention the countless potential highline locations.

After all my amazing travels to North America, it was almost as if my accumulated experience was out of balance. Like when I lean too far in one direction on the line and at some point need a balancing impulse to the other side to finally find my center again. This was the case with my slackline adventures, but also with my intercultural experiences. At some point I was drawn toward the east.

The easternmost place I have ever been to was not in Asia but in Australia. A wonderful slackline trip to the Blue Mountains, where I met my old friends Jerry, Mia, and Aidan again. Aidan showed us his home in Sydney, the Outback, Down Under, kangaroos, and koalas. And even though I walked over 30 different highlines on the Red Continent and became great friends with the incredibly laid-back, young Aussie slackline community at the Blue Mountains Highline Gathering, there is unfortunately not enough space in this book to report on this trip in detail.

It is the same with India. In January 2020, the Indian slackline community invited me to the Great Indian Highline Gathering in Lonavala, Maharashtra, to set the Indian highline record together. Getting to know these super-friendly people and balancing 4,590 feet / 1,400 meters in one go in the middle of the night under the Indian full moon were unforgettable experiences that I would like to describe in more detail. Likewise, there was a painful contrast between slums, poverty, and crowds on the one hand, and magnificent skyscrapers and luxury holiday apartments on the other.

And then, of course, there was China. I was lucky enough to travel to the Middle Kingdom three times. Each time, it was a tightly organized trip from start to finish, centered around a highline competition broadcast on Chinese state television to boost domestic tourism. I saw breathtakingly beautiful nature on one side and smog-polluted cities with millions of inhabitants on the other. The futuristic skyline of Shanghai and Buddhist temples. Hospitality and curiosity as well as secrecy and aloofness. It was a privilege to see this distant, foreign, yet so present country up close.

But the time there was short, the travel regulations strict, and the experiences not profound enough to write a detailed chapter about them with a clear conscience. I would only be scratching the surface, and that wouldn't be fair. I want to dedicate the following chapter to a country that I can now honestly say I have gotten to know firsthand.

Russia

KISLOVODSK, RUSSIA
2018

I can't remember ever being as excited about a trip as I was before my first trip to Russia in May 2018.

Russia . . . the largest country in the world. Eleven time zones, four oceans, and fourteen neighboring countries. Tundra in the north, taiga in the middle, steppes and deserts in the south. Temperatures from -94°F / -70°C to 113°F / 45°C in the same country. Polar bears, moose, wolves, and tigers. Icebergs and volcanoes. Oil rigs, pipelines, gigantic mines, and magnificent, power-celebrating cities like Moscow and Saint Petersburg. Tsarist Empire, Communist Superpower, Oligarchy. True stuff of legends. I was fascinated by this infamous yet legendary outsider among the great countries of the world. I just had to see for myself.

Thursday, 4/26/2018

A short stopover in Moscow, then landing at the tiny airport of *Mineralnye Vody* (tiny mineral water), a medium-sized city in the Northern

Caucasus foothills, a good 1,300 kilometers [810 miles] south of Moscow.

Immediately after landing, Sasha picks me up. His first words to me: "Hey Frrrrriedi, hurrry up dude, my carrr is waiting in no parrrk zone," with a crazy Russian accent and the most rolled *r* I have ever heard. Not even my grandfather could roll the *r* like that.

On the car journey to Kislovodsk, a city even further south, I see for the first time the highest mountain in Europe, the snow-white Elbrus, rising monstrously from the landscape. First stop: a super-cool, colorful farmers market with fruit, vegetables, exotic sweets, nuts, cheese, pastries, and friendly vendors who, of course, speak zero English. Then we arrive at the highline festival site on the edge of a beautiful canyon with an idyllic babbling river, tents on the edge of the forest, and a huge fire pit.

We rig 90 meters [300 feet] of highline on the bouncy lift webbing that I brought with me. Sasha makes the first attempt and loves it. Meanwhile, I walk all seven other lines of the festival, which are up to 200 meters [660 feet] long.

In the evening, a wonderful campfire atmosphere with the super hospitable slackliners, who somehow already won me over. Tea, biscuits, dates, and stew with potatoes and beef cooked over the

```
campfire. Afterward, beautifully sad-sounding
Russian songs around the campfire with guitar
accompaniment.
```

After my first night in the tent, the next day greeted me with wonderful sunny spring weather. I felt more like I was in the South of France than in Russia. And no wonder: The spa town of Kislovodsk, with its 128,000 inhabitants and known for its natural mineral baths, lies at roughly the same latitude as Marseille.

At breakfast, I met Gennadi "Genna" Skripko, the oldest active highliner I know. He's fifty-five years old and proud of the fact that he still works as an artist and jack-of-all-trades in the circus, and in his free time runs highlines up to 660 feet / 200 meters long. Although we could only communicate in a makeshift way, with my few scraps of Russian, which I had taught myself with Duolingo before the trip, and his sparse English, we quickly became friends. We admired each other's strengths and knew we could learn a lot from each other.

He sped along with Sasha, me, and a few other slackliners in his old, rickety Lada jeep through run-down villages, over hills and fields, all the way to the other side of the gorge. The term *redneck* actually describes a typical American country bumpkin, but somehow it seemed appropriate here too.

Only once did another car come toward us. I saw a boy peeking out from behind the steering wheel who could barely have been twelve years old. Once we reached the other side, we spent several hours clearing a hillside of trash and debris before we finally reached the rock. Genna drilled the anchor for what was then Russia's longest highline. Setting up the 890-foot-long / 270-meter-long line the next day proved rather difficult, as is often the case when not everyone on the team speaks the same language. I could tell that Sasha and Genna were equally keen on this little highline milestone and would surely compete to see who would be the first to walk it.

But when two fight, a third one wins: After the two had crossed it with several catches each, and I had assured myself that they wouldn't mind if I managed the first ascent, I went to the line and onsighted it full man. This encouraged and inspired the other slackliners to push themselves even harder. In the following days, the two of them eventually managed to complete the full route and together they thought of a name for the line, although I don't remember it anymore.

The most fun for me came in the evening: Sasha (who works as an event technician in his normal life) set up two huge speakers powered by diesel generators, as well as a DJ booth and all kinds of disco lights, very close to the anchor point of the new line. The highline rave party could begin.

The approximately seventy festival visitors started dancing while I balanced on the 890-foot / 270-meter highline into the darkness. When I heard the sound of the river directly below me, I turned around and got goosebumps. Before my walk on the line, Sasha agreed to play my favorite playlist of techno and trance music. An unconscious dream came true. I didn't see the line, but I felt the vibrations as I balanced toward dancing figures in the flickering glow of campfires and disco lights. The pounding, dark rhythm of the techno music grew louder with every step. Balancing had become my dance. Above me the stars, below me the abyss, in front of me my newly made friends. That was real life.

Sunday, 4/29/2018

The guys and girls of the "NO FEAR Extreme team" have a great hobby and profession: rigging giant rope jumps over ravines. One jump costs 1,500 rubles, the equivalent of just under 20 dollars. Ridiculous price for all that effort.

Gaining recognition from the NO FEAR team is pretty straightforward. You must not show any fear before your jump, you must not hesitate for a second when taking off, and it is best to laugh while doing so and shout some dirty Russian swear word after "Three, two, one, zero." So be it.

But I'm not completely without fear, and so my tucked gainer becomes a bit crooked and timid. Afterward, there is still an *"Ahuien"* from above (Russian for something like cock-horny or ass-horny).

After rope jumping and a nap in the hammock, a short session on the 90-meter [30-foot] line and then, goal achieved, a 550-meter [1,800-foot] continuous walk on the 270-meter [890-foot] line. Ready for 1km+ [over half a mile] highlines!

Dinner at the campfire: buckwheat with tomatoes and chicken.

Afterward, the big speakers are set up again and while a perfect golden full moon slowly rises behind the mountain range, Russian hippies dance to energetic progressive psytrance music. Guys and girls spin fire poi and other burning toys to the driving rhythm. Happiness cannot be put into words.

I can't stay in one place for too long. I was drawn to Mount Elbrus. Saying goodbye to the festival took over an hour because everyone wanted to take selfies with me. When I finally got into the car with the slackline couple, Vova and Anya, I was completely exhausted, had sunstroke, and slept most of the way. We drove for hours through beautiful villages, over hills and through valleys, surrounded by mountain meadows full of cows and sheep and, little by little, snow.

Finally, we arrived in the cute mountain hotel village of Azau at 7,870 feet / 2,400 meters above sea level, which reminded me of El Chaltén in Chile, where I visited with my grandfather in 2011. We slept at the Hotel Meridian, where some German and Austrian participants of the Red Fox Elbrus Race were also staying. The Elbrus Race is an international skyrunning competition in which some of the fittest and craziest mountain runners in the world race to the top of Europe's highest peak and back again as fast as possible. Red Fox is Russia's largest brand for outdoor clothing and equipment, and supported my trip financially at the time.

What You See Is What You Get

The next day, after a small, somewhat rushed breakfast, it was time to check the location. I was grateful for my experienced companions.

Vladimir Murzaev, nicknamed "Vova," is two years older than me and a true all-round extreme sports athlete: alpine climbing, BASE jumping, and, more recently, highlining are among his specialties. Anya had been slacklining for many years and had helped Sasha organize the festival.

The thin air at an altitude of almost 9,840 feet / 3,000 meters made us gasp with every step. Plus, it was below fifty degrees Fahrenheit / ten degrees Celsius. We finally found a suitable spot for a nearly 330-foot-long / 100-meter-long line, right above the ski slope that the race participants would be racing up the next day. Now that we knew what we could rig, we descended the 1,310 feet / 400 meters to the hotel to tape the line and get the necessary equipment.

When we made the second ascent to the highline spot in the early afternoon, we could no longer find the boulder we had chosen as an anchor, nor the small daypack I had left there with my climbing harness, Grigri, a few highline slings, food, and drink. . . . Everything had been buried by a huge, slow-moving avalanche. Where we stood a few hours ago, there was only a thick layer of hard, partly icy snow and mud. There was no question of digging it out. We didn't even know exactly where the anchor point was. Thank God we weren't there when the avalanche happened.

Our mood adapted to the temperature and our stress levels rose. The next morning my highline show was scheduled to take place. It was already afternoon, and we could start looking for a location all over again. I noticed that my body was sending me signals. Now it was time to rest, but we couldn't afford that.

After much exploration and discussion, we were forced to settle on a questionable alternative line between two old, rusty ski lift masts. We secured them as best we could to the rear—to other rusty structures that were half-protruding from the snow. "You have to take what you can get." There is definitely a similar saying in Russian.

Finally we had the line set up and I did a test walk with my last reserves. The line wobbled endlessly because it wasn't taut enough. After we had solved this problem and were able to descend, it was already dark and bitterly cold.

While waiting for dinner in the small living room, I began to tremble slightly. I could barely eat a bite of my chicken and rice, even though my stomach had been growling all day. Insanely, I was still careful not to let the other guests in the room notice anything. Among them was Susanne, the German marketing manager of Red Fox, to whom I had told that morning that everything was going perfectly according to plan and that I would be doing a fantastic highline show the next day. With great difficulty I got up from the table and dragged myself up the stairs. My plan was to collapse into bed in my room, but I was already shivering so badly that I was scared. I knocked tremblingly on Anya and Vova's door.

When they opened the door, I was just a miserable little heap that fell into their arms. I could hardly speak, mumbled something like: "I'm fucked, guys."

The two of them helped me onto their bed and immediately wrapped me in blankets. They lay down next to me to warm me with their bodies and spoke kindly to me, but the shivering and shaking just didn't stop. I had never felt so exhausted in my life before, and I wondered if I would suffer permanent damage, if I had permanently ruined myself . . .

Anya and Vova told me that they had experienced something like this before and that what I needed most now was warmth and sugar.

My blood sugar level was at rock bottom, so they first gave me all the chocolate and sweets they could find in the room. I could only chew with difficulty and swallow tiny bites, still shivering despite the warm room and the many blankets.

Vova quickly ran downstairs to get hot tea and hot chocolate. They poured almost another handful of sugar into the drinks, and I sipped them. I cried a little because I felt so much pity for my own body, which I had demanded so much from. Why? Maybe I also cried because I was so touched by the helpfulness and care of the two Russian slackliners. I had known them for less than two weeks, but Anya was caring for me like a mother.

At some point the shaking subsided, I calmed down, breathed more slowly, and felt the warmth return to my limbs. I managed to drink more and more of the hot chocolate—and that helped.

At some point I fell asleep. . . .

At the end of this chapter in my diary, it says: "Take better care of yourself. Listen to your body."

The Show Must Go On

Despite my exhaustion, I got up early and, in the icy wind, performed a short highline show above the ski slope at an altitude of 9,190 feet / 2,800 meters, all for the participants, spectators, and organizers of the Red Fox Elbrus Race 2018. When the starting gun went off, however, I was back at the bottom, admiring the tough men and women from all over the world running up Mount Elbrus toward the summit, some of them faster than I would jog on flat terrain at home! These people were wiry, fit, and determined. One thing was clear—they knew how to listen to their bodies. Or their bodies simply obeyed them in every situation . . .

As the runners, including Vlad, the owner of Red Fox, disappeared over the horizon, I made my way to the cable car to follow Susanne. From the gondola we saw how the young Austrian, Dominik, who was about my age, was already a good 330 feet / 100 meters ahead of the other mountain runners and was building up more and more of a lead. What an animal!

At the station at 12,800 feet / 3,900 meters, I boarded a huge snowcat, the back of which was full of reporters and other freaks who weren't taking part in the race but were still involved. Again, that redneck vibe came up, which I had experienced in Russia in a similar way to that years before in the US. The two countries have much more in common than you might think.

We all clung to something while the snowcat sped up the slopes. I didn't understand a word of what was being said or shouted around me. We stopped at an altitude of almost 17,060 feet / 5,200 meters. Since the summit was closed due to strong winds and difficult snow conditions, we had to wait at the finish line surrounded by banners. Apparently, some athletes were already close to the summit. There they were met by only a few jury members who checked whether the summit had actually been reached. The competitors were supposed to turn around immediately and run down to an altitude of 17,060 feet / 5,200 meters, where the race ended.

I walked around a bit, realizing how exhausting it is at this altitude with thick clothes and heavy snow. Somewhere I found a flat surface for a handstand photo and did my highest handstand to date!

Then I heard the first shouts and realized that the fastest runners, all tracked by GPS, had already reached the summit and were on their way to us. Dominik was still leading.

Just minutes later, he crossed the finish line, tearing apart a plastic ribbon that had been hung there. He cheered, panted, and sweated despite the cold—and yet he seemed as if he could keep running forever.

After a few more runners arrived, there was tea and borscht for them, the photographers, and the outsider who was just watching—that's me—in a cozy, warm hut filled with smoke from a wood-burning stove.

Afterward, we went back to the valley for the award ceremony. My Russian friends and I walked across the line again for fun. When we had dismantled everything, the last participants of the race slowly trickled in. They were mostly older, some over fifty or sixty years old, and seemed significantly more exhausted than those who were faster. Still absolutely crazy. As quickly as possible from 9,840 to 18,510 feet / 3,000 to 5,642 meters above sea level and back again. Over hill and dale and ice and snow. The idea of running myself one day began to appeal to me . . .

In the evening I had a little chat with Dominik, the unexpected winner of the race. He told me that as a child he always walked through the mountains in Austria. You could see it in his calves. And his shining eyes as well. Mountain running seemed to give him the same feeling that highlining gave me.

The next morning we tried again in vain to dig out my harness and backpack from the avalanche from the day before yesterday. It didn't help. One of the Russians from the small mountain village said he would wait until the snow melted in midsummer and look for it, and if he found anything, he would send it to Vlad in Saint Petersburg.

Then it was time to say goodbye to Mount Elbrus because my flight to Saint Petersburg was the next day. On the way back to Mineralni Vody, I once again enjoyed the view of the beautiful, wild landscape, which was not so dissimilar to the Alps. I saw the peaks and mountain ranges and dreamed of what gigantic alpine highlines one could create here if only one returned with more time, a larger team, and the right equipment. I was exhausted and happy. The journey had already given me everything I had hoped for, and it wasn't even over yet.

Saint Petersburg

After a short photography presentation at the Red Fox Flag Store in the heart of Saint Petersburg, with a slackline workshop and mini slackline show, I met Katya, who had worked as a Russian foreign language assistant at Lewis & Clark College in Portland at the same time that I worked there. She didn't know much about slacklining and wilderness adventures. But she was very happy to show me her magnificent hometown. We visited the Hermitage Museum, looked at rivers, tsarist palaces and parks, and went out for a fancy Georgian meal in the evening. We reminisced about our time in the US.

Those were nice moments, but like a magnet, I was still drawn back to other slackliners. Kolya, the owner of Souz Slacklines, the only Russian slackline company, lived his profession: Instead of living in a nice apartment, he lived in his tiny workshop, which he had rented in an old, abandoned factory site, surrounded by band rehearsal rooms, broken glass, and underground parties. Of course we immediately rigged a highline between the ancient, dilapidated brick buildings. Funny: One moment I had to protect my slackline from ice and snow, and the next moment from dust, broken glass, and pigeon droppings.

"This factory is more than *100* years old and closed for sixty years now," Kolya told me. We climbed up to the roof through half-broken stairwells and fire escapes, did a few handstands in a pose, and jumped from roof to roof wherever we could. Parkour moves like in my youth.

Time flew by and suddenly the last day arrived. At the airport, with tears of joy, I wrote the last words in my diary. They ended with the name of the Russian rope jump team, which had somehow become the motto of the whole trip:

"It's unbelievable how underestimated this country is, what it has to offer and what amazing friends I've made here in just three weeks. NO FEAR."

Moscow City Urban World Record

There has been talk about my top three or top five highlines before, and I think it has become clear that being close to nature has always played a big role for me. But one of the top three couldn't have been further from nature and wilderness: the 720-foot-long / 220-meter-long and 1,150-foot-high / 350-meter-high line between the OKO and Neva skyscrapers in downtown Moscow—the Guinness Highline World Record for the highest highline ever walked in an urban area.

The Moscow slackline community, which also includes Sasha, Vova, and Anya, whom I had met at the festival a year earlier, invited some international reinforcements for this record, including Mia Noblet and me. The whole thing is pretty fancy. Even a referee from the Guinness Book of Records was on hand to register this new world record and present us with certificates. The line reminded me strongly of the film *Man on Wire* about the French tightrope walker Philippe Petit, who illegally balanced between the towers of the World Trade Center in New York in 1974 and thereby achieved worldwide fame.

My personal highlight of this event was walking the line at night. I almost felt like I was in a video game. One thousand one hundred fifty feet / three hundred fifty meters below me, the people and cars shrank to the size of ants. Instead of mountains, there were only houses around me as far as the eye could see, and yet I was floating above it all, all alone. An electrifying feeling. Looking closely, I saw figures behind the windows of the huge office towers waving at me or frantically taking photos with their cell phones. What could be going on in their heads?

Reflection

Not all experiences in Russia were successful. In the city of Perm, the last real big city before the Ural Mountains, we rigged a half-a-mile-long highline for a big city festival, but it was so low that it had to be redirected using several cranes. A completely absurd rigging challenge, one that certainly taught me a lot, and one of my greatest live shows to date, but it almost cost me my life. During the dismantling, we were under so much time pressure, poorly prepared, and short of staff that somehow Vova and I ended up on top of a crane with our hands cut by ropes and webbing, our faces covered in chain grease, and our clothes completely soaked by the rain, when suddenly a damn thunderstorm broke out above us. I remember all too well Vova staring at me with his eyes wide open and his mouth open, his face brightly lit by a flash of lightning that probably struck less than 160 feet / 50 meters away. We even felt a burst of warmth for a moment!

"Let's go down right now and fix this shit later. It's not worth it," Vova said to me.

It didn't take much to convince me. I had never rappelled down anything so quickly before. We were cutting it close. The phrase "What doesn't kill you makes you stronger" cannot be extended indefinitely.

Another time, the whole event literally fell through. The city of Samara hired us to set a one-mile waterline world record across the Volga. When I arrived there again with the same friends—Vova, Anya, Kolya, and Sasha—we discovered that corners had been cut and none of the technicians on site had listened to our instructions regarding the necessary preparation. We were still forced to try. In short: It ended with several hundred feet of my high-tech slackline, which I had brought with me from Germany, being shredded by a ship's propeller and now rotting away somewhere on the bottom of the Volga.

There was no world record attempt. The event was canceled at the last minute and the organizers tried to blame us slackliners and even wanted to extort financial compensation from us for the botched event. It stank of mafia and corruption. I felt so uneasy several times during the whole process that I became really sick. In the end, we were able to wriggle out of the situation with great difficulty and at least got paid for the lost material.

But I'm sure heads were still rolling higher up in the Russian event business hierarchy. Here too, I swore to myself: never again. From now on, only events with 100 percent transparent communication, clear contracts, and no last-minute decisions.

The current political developments in Russia today, as I write these lines, break my heart, to say the least, and I do not know when or if I will ever see the friends I have grown so fond of there again. I have long since lost contact with my former sponsor, Red Fox, and I only have very sporadic contact with the Russian slackliners via social media. Some of them have left the country. I do not want to let my beautiful memories be spoiled by a dark present, especially since the story is not yet over.

My Second Russian Highline Festival, Kislovodsk, 2019

Since last year, an incredible amount of development has taken place here in Kislovodsk. The 890-foot / 270-meter course from last year was now used by several guys and girls, just as a dozen new lines were set up. Many were freestyle highlining, doing Yoda rolls, which had been the most difficult trick there was just a year ago. There was a speedline competition, which I was lucky enough to win. Lukas, who was part of the race this time, had to deal with the wind during his turn on the line and therefore had to walk slower than usual. Aidan had also fulfilled a long-held dream and joined us from Australia.

The highlight of the entire festival was the 3,280-foot-long / 1,000-meter-long highline, which is still the longest in Russia. Setting it up was comparatively easy thanks to many helping hands and a rigging-friendly location—a meadow valley about 660 feet / 200 meters deep with sheep pastures and only a few trees and rocks. Running the line was a bit more challenging but not rocket science. Lukas and I both succeeded on our first attempt in good conditions. A few days later, Jaan Rose from Estonia also succeeded and, after many persistent attempts, Sasha and finally Genna. Everyone was happy with that. The two alpha dogs of the local highline scene had completed the line, setting a new Russian record, and Lukas and I were able to use the line as training for even greater distances.

But as is the case with us slacklifers, we always want to go one step further. After walking back to the middle of my second ascent, turning around at the end and trying to increase my speed more and more, I thought for the first time about crossing the line blind. After all, that would be a potential new world record, and you can never have enough of those. The near failure on the 2,920-foot-long / 890-meter-long line in Utah six months earlier was still haunting me. Maybe now was the time to strike back? It would be tough, that much was clear. The thought made me nervous, so I used a tried-and-tested strategy: simply telling myself that I just wanted to see how far I could get. I wasn't seriously considering the entire send or even the world record. This works particularly well when the external conditions, usually the weather, are bad anyway, which was the case at that time because there were more and more gusts of wind.

I said to myself, "Okay, another whole crossing won't work now anyway, but I still have energy, so I'll just see how far I can get blind."

After a short break, I slid back out onto the line, pulled my buff over my eyes, and carefully stood up. And it was . . . easier than expected. At least the start. I was well trained and ready to chase the blind highline world record after two years.

I got almost to the middle with just two or three catches. But the gusts of wind were getting stronger, and I decided to cross back as fast as possible without a blindfold to rest for a later attempt in better conditions. I was hooked. I understood the line blindfolded. It was doable.

Mind Cinema

By late afternoon of the same day, the wind had mostly calmed down and the line was hanging in the air with only a slight, steady side-sag. So I put on my buff and got started. Aidan, Lukas, Sasha, and some other Russian slackliners were chilling at the anchor behind me and wishing me good luck.

This time I started much closer to the anchor, just far enough away that if I dropped the leash, I wouldn't swing against the wall. This made the first steps much more difficult, and I had to walk extremely slowly in the first few meters and fight to avoid falling. But I wanted it to truly count, should it, contrary to expectations, become a full ascent. But I still didn't want to seriously think about it.

"It's just for fun, let's see how far I get this time," I had said to my friends before. That was a lie. I wanted to trick myself again, take the pressure off myself, not get my hopes up too much, so that I would be less disappointed if I failed. But deep down, I dreamed of sending the line and finally breaking the blind highline world record.

After a tough start of maybe 100, 130, or 160 feet / 30, 40, or 50 meters, who knows when you can't see anything, the line finally became easier. I decided to use a tried and tested strategy: I played poker.

I told myself, "Fuck what happens, just try to get through the first few hundred meters as fast as you can, even if your walk is sloppy and unsteady. If you fall, not much is lost because you haven't put much energy into fighting yet. But if you're lucky and don't fall, you'll have come a long way with relatively little effort and can go slower later when it really counts."

The strategy worked! Even though I could never say exactly how far I had gone, I was aware of the high speed with which I was taking my steps and that quite a bit of time had passed since I had started crossing. Things were no longer noticeably downhill. I had to be somewhere in the middle of the line, maybe even further. I hadn't had any real fights since the beginning and still felt more than fit enough to keep walking. But now the real mental challenge gradually forced its way into my thoughts. I was invested. The world record was at stake. Suddenly, "I don't care if you fall" was no longer an option. And was I mistaken or were those gusts of wind causing the line beneath me to vibrate more and more in unpredictable, jerky ways? Why now again? It was enough to make you cry. So the window of good conditions was over, and I had no idea how far I still had to balance.

But I kept going. It wasn't long before I started cursing and fighting. At the same time, I was happy that my initial poker game had worked and that I still had some energy reserves. I realized more and more that I would need it urgently, that I would probably have to give this line everything I had. Couldn't it be easy to set a world record at least once? On the other hand, what would the title be worth if you didn't have to fight a little for it? What would anything in life be worth if it were free? I thought of the wise words of my friend Pablo: "Don't be afraid to really commit to the send. You either walk, or you give up."

My shoulders and arms were now burning from holding the line for so long and from the intense, sometimes jerky balancing movements that I needed, especially when the wind was shaking the line particularly hard, and I didn't notice it until very late due to a lack of visibility. And whenever it got quiet, I tried to walk a little faster, although not nearly as fast and sloppily as at the beginning, because there was something at stake now.

At least twice I almost slipped on one of the connections covered with adhesive tape or had to stop suddenly because the leash ring got caught there. I screamed loudly and cursed every time, even though I knew deep down that it wouldn't help and that my chances were better the less I got caught up in my emotions.

It felt like I had been on the trail for a very long time, and I thought I could already feel a hint of incline in the line. There it was again, the heightened alertness of one sense due to the loss of another. With each step, my front foot touched the line a little earlier, probably only millimeters, but I felt it. That meant I had already walked well over halfway, probably already in the last quarter of the line. Maybe the end was closer than I thought. But it didn't make my situation any easier. The wind gusts were strong, possibly due to the stepped terrain under the last few hundred meters of the line, which caused the winds channeled through the valley to bounce off and redirect upwards.

The increasing proximity of the anchor made the vibrations of the line more jerky. It felt less and less like half-a-mile-long highline and more like a tightly stretched longline. Added to this was the creeping thought that I couldn't see the end, so I was in danger of swinging against the wall at some point during the leash fall. It's really crazy what horror scenarios you sometimes play in your head when highlining, especially when you're blindfolded and completely alone with your thoughts. I can't remember every detail of my mental rollercoaster ride, but I know that I absolutely gave it my all in the last three hundred feet / hundred meters. I had fought so hard and expected to fall at any moment, but somehow, I held on to my last bit of balance. I screamed, cursed, sweated, and trembled, but somehow, I still managed to take another step. I just didn't want to fail again so close to the end like I did a year earlier in the US.

It was now going so steeply uphill that it really couldn't be far anymore. I wish there had been people at the anchor in front of me who could have cheered me on and, above all, shouted to me how far I still had to go. But I was all alone with my mindfuck. At some point, when it got so steep that I was terrified of hurting myself, I stopped, shifted my weight onto my back foot, exhaled, and very carefully and slowly pushed the blindfold up a bit. The piercing brightness of the daylight almost overwhelmed me. There was a slackline band below me, against a green-brown background, and, NO, that couldn't be true, the wall was not THIRTY feet / TEN meters in front of me!

The weblock, the slings, the anchor, the end of my odyssey lay before me. "Don't give it away now," I told myself. I slowly pulled the buff back over my eyes and decided to take exactly ten more steps, sit down, and only then take the blindfold off again. Then the line would be considered as being sent. Those ten steps truly felt like an eternity. I don't know if my arms had ever burned like this, or if I had ever been so bent to my knees. I just wanted to get my center of gravity as close to the line as possible to gain stability, even though I could barely feel my legs anymore. When I finally, after the tenth step, began to sit down almost in slow motion, before my hand finally touched the webbing, I heard shouts of joy from the distance behind me, and even in the valley below me. Thank God. The others had noticed that I had walked to the end. I was only cheering inwardly. I just had no energy left.

When I took off the blindfold, it was only six to ten feet / two to three meters to the end, the no-fall zone, where it is customary to sit down beforehand for safety reasons. But even bridging this short distance by hanging and sliding was something I only managed with great difficulty. I didn't even have the strength to sit down, let alone stand up, so I simply let myself fall onto the small rock plateau and closed my eyes while lying down.

It still took me some time to get used to the brightness. I was empty and drained. I was drenched in sweat and my throat was dry and sore from all the screaming. I wanted to cheer, but still no sound came out of my lips. I felt more like sleeping. It was strange to arrive at an empty anchor after a world record attempt, without the hugs and congratulations of others. I decided to capture the moment somehow anyway and took a short selfie video describing what I had done and briefly filming the line and surroundings. My hair was completely messed up, my eyes were watery, and I barely had a voice left. But I had managed to cover half a mile blind as the first slackliner in the world and would at least be able to share the final moment with the community later.

Ten or fifteen minutes later, a little strength had returned to my limbs, and my desire for real company and hugs, but also for water, was so great that I set out to run back through the Wiesental Valley to my friends. On the way, I quickly washed myself in a small stream and lay down on the ground next to it in the middle of a flower meadow. Beside me the music of the water, cows grazing on the other bank, above me a bright blue sky through which stretched a line gently swaying in the wind. Close to despair less than an hour ago. Now a feeling of happy exhaustion, idyll, and security. Such contrasts are the spice of life.

The next day, Lukas also managed to walk the line blind. Like me, it took him about fifty minutes, and he certainly went through his own psychological ups and downs. We celebrated the whole team's success together around the campfire. And thanks to Lukas' good connection to Guinness World Records, we received an entry in the Book of Records and, a few months later, a certificate for the "longest blindfolded highline ascent." And even though it's not hanging on my wall, I'm still happy every time I hold it in my hand to have this tangible and official reminder of the Russian highline festival.

The Road Trip of My Life

RUSSIAN-GEORGIAN BORDER CROSSING AT THE TEREK
EARLY MAY 2019

Georgia

Soon after the half-a-mile project, the festival also came to an end. Lukas got his ride back to the airport while Sasha, Vova, Jaan, Aidan, and I embarked on the road trip of a lifetime.

The journey from Russia to Georgia, over gigantic mountain passes in the Caucasus, reminded me a bit of the Brenner Pass between Germany and Italy. Except that the mountains here were much higher and rougher. At the top of the pass it was colder and there was 1.5 feet / 0.5 meters of snow. The trucks also seemed much larger and more beastly, again a parallel to the United States. The border buildings appeared cold and threatening, flanked by many armed border police officers, some of whom checked our passports with grim expressions. But nevertheless, just like at the Brenner Pass, we drove from the colder north to the warmer south, crossed a breathtakingly beautiful mountain range and thus entered one of the Russians' favorite holiday destinations: Georgia.

At the highest point of the mountain road—at over 9,850 feet / 3,000 meters above sea level—we took a photo of Sasha's van, which had never climbed so high before. During the breaks, we made coffee and *gretschka* (buckwheat) on the gas stove in the van. Aidan in particular was completely fed up with this dish, but it was filling and is said to have saved entire nations from starvation. The sight of the mountains around us left me speechless. In my memory, the peaks of the Alps seemed puny in comparison. Instead of chic motorway restaurants, the rest stops here were more likely to feature old chapels, dilapidated farms, and mountain streams where those resting filled up their water canisters.

Georgia's Longest Highline

Our first highline attempt in Georgia was doomed to failure. We had seen photos online of the 130-foot-high / forty-meter-high iconic rock needle, the Katskhi Pillar, about 330 feet / 100 meters from an equally high rock face with a picturesque monastery at its base and a small monastery building on top of the needle. It was said that an ancient Georgian monk lived there for several decades and that he never came down from the rock needle in all that time so he could stay as close to God as possible. Using a rickety, hand-operated cable, his monks sent him food and water up in wooden buckets every day. Our idea was to rig a highline to this famous rock needle, which is photographed by tourists every day. But what a surprise: the monks were not convinced of our plan, even after Sasha talked to them in his usual military-aggressive tone and gestured about how professional we were and that we wouldn't be able to knock down the rock needle with our band.

The alternative that soon presented itself made up for everything. As we were once again searching the map for possible highline spots not far from our route, we came across the old mining town of Chiatura, a town in the middle of a valley, surrounded by steep, hundreds-of-meters-high cliffs, full of ancient Soviet-era mines where manganese and iron ore were once mined. In pictures we saw that old cable cars were hanging everywhere. This place was crying out for a highline.

Once there, we drove around, munching on buttery local khachapuri, until we discovered a side canyon that was about 980 feet / 300 meters wide and 660 feet / 200 meters high. Back home in Germany, what we did next would have been unthinkable. We simply drove the van along muddy gravel roads to the edge of the gorge and happily started setting up our highline, even though there was a road running along the bottom of the gorge. On one side we used a thick tree as an anchor point, and on the other side we wrapped ourselves around several rusty but thick steel pipes of unidentifiable structures that protruded from the ground. The few people who saw us didn't pay any attention to us. More than half of the surrounding prefabricated buildings, surrounded by jungle, appeared to be uninhabited and in a very dilapidated state anyway.

After Jaan had flown the fishing line over with the drone, it took less than an hour until we had pulled up the line and tightened it. It was clear to us that we would soon receive a visit, at the latest when one of us would be balancing through the air at a height of 660 feet / 200 meters, only a few hundred yards from the center of Chiatura. So we quickly set about walking this line. A huge pleasure!

Sasha and Jaan each made it on their second attempt, Vova crossed the line with a few catches, and I walked it back and forth several times on my first attempt. I stopped in the middle and looked and observed the old mining town from a bird's-eye view. I could even see people in the city center, the view from up there was so good.

Soon, the first locals arrived to watch the spectacle up close. A man of about fifty to sixty years old with a tanned, bearded and constantly smiling face was the first to speak to us—and he even spoke in German. His name was Mikayel. He was thrilled with our show and soon returned to us with bread, wine, and pickled vegetables. He also had his whole family in tow, who watched us fascinated.

But the police arrived soon after. The first uniformed officer who showed up grinned from ear to ear and thought what we were doing was super cool. His colleagues, who arrived shortly afterward, were somewhat less amused, but quickly engaged in conversation with the other locals and showed little desire to do anything to stop us. Especially since we could hardly communicate with them. They seemed to be waiting.

We soon found out why. A man arrived who I wouldn't have recognized as a police officer if Mikayel hadn't told me. He was younger and slimmer than the others and wore a fine jacket instead of a uniform and weapon. He was apparently a kind of police chief of this region and had arrived quickly from the nearest larger city. He was not at all enthusiastic about our little project and told us in a very annoyed tone that the highline had to be dismantled immediately. He couldn't tell us why it had to be dismantled.

Of course we had previously discussed that we would always make the changeovers as quick and our sessions as comfortable and extended as possible, so that the line was always occupied.

We had Mikayel translate our usual excuses for the police chief: "It's too windy to take down the line now. . . . We have to balance across again to retrieve an important part. . . . It's too dangerous to distract the balancer now. . . . We're setting a new highline record in Georgia. . . . One last attempt, please. . . ." and so on and so on. In addition, the now numerous spectators were constantly talking to the police officers—apparently in our favor. All while Vova enjoyed another walk on the highline, waving to the spectators every now and then, and pushing himself further and further on the highline, which was still relatively long for him.

The police chief spoke to someone on the phone every few minutes and seemed increasingly frustrated. Then a reporter arrived with a camera crew. They had received a cell phone photo two hours earlier and had then rushed out of the capital, Tbilisi, to film these exotic slackline pilgrims in their balancing act. They interviewed Sasha and me, took their pictures, and made the whole event seem even more spectacular for the locals.

At some point, the smartly dressed police chief left us after extracting a promise from us that we would dismantle the line before dark. He left one of his subordinates with us as a guard. Visibly unhappy, he sat grumpily on a bench for the rest of the day, smoking a cigarette, while we made the most of the highline, enjoyed the applause of the locals, and finally dismantled the line in the last light of day.

Armenia

I had never seen such a look of fear on Aidan's face. Our road trip was supposed to take us from Georgia to Armenia, and after waiting for hours in a line of cars, a grim, camouflage-wearing border guard with a machine gun slung over his shoulder came to our car at the border with the neighboring country and demanded our papers. He looked at our passports one by one and disrespectfully threw them back into the car. At Aidan's Australian passport, he paused briefly and tried to pronounce Aidan's name, relatively unsuccessfully.

He looked at the then twenty-one-year-old with a dark expression, formed a gun with his thumb and index finger, pointed it at Aidan, and said, "Bang!" He let out a loud, nasty laugh.

Aidan's face was pale, and he clearly wanted nothing more than to get out of this situation unscathed as quickly as possible. Nobody said anything. We hadn't done anything wrong, but border guards are just good at making people feel guilty. After a long, awkward silence, in which our minds raced but we couldn't utter a word, the guy finally waved us on. What a relief!

Soon after, we were able to laugh a little at the shock that was still written on Aidan's face.

The Vintage Cars

Since Sasha didn't want anyone else to drive his bus, the rest of our gang had plenty of time to study the route ahead of us in more detail on Google Maps. Vova's focus was not only on highline locations, but also on potential BASE exits. He had his parachute with him.

At some point he read about a very interesting object on a blog: the largest railway bridge in Armenia. A giant steel monster from Soviet times, stretched over a 460-foot-deep / 140-meter-deep canyon through which the Hrazdan River flowed. It wouldn't be a big detour, so we set off.

Once we got there, we quickly realized that the bridge was guarded: Rocking on a rocking chair in front of a small, dilapidated guardhouse at the beginning of the bridge sat a funny-looking, elderly, sun-tanned man wearing sweatpants, slippers, a camouflage T-shirt, and with a Kalashnikov slung over his shoulders. As we approached him, a huge grin spread across his face. Communication with him was somewhat easier because, especially among the elderly, almost all people in Armenia speak Russian. And so Sasha and Vova not only managed to explain to the old Armenian what a highline is, they even managed to get him excited about it. He said he still had to talk to his chief officer, but that he thought it would be cool if we balanced in the air here next to the bridge.

The boss, whom I would soon meet in person, gave us permission and we were even allowed to walk across the bridge with the tagline in our hands to establish our connection. With this and a compensating anchor between several bushes on one side and a wrapped stable ruin on the other side, our highline was set up after an hour. It was 951 feet / 290 meters long, making it the longest highline in Armenia.

Sasha got the first attempt again and after a few falls on the way there, he managed to walk the whole way back and thus finally send one of our lines for the first time, which made the whole team very happy.

My walk then became the ultimate odyssey. After I had traversed the onsight full man line, I walked back to the middle armed with a

GoPro and selfie stick to film Vova doing his BASE jump from the bridge. In all seriousness, the daredevil did a forward somersault on his very first jump and landed easily on a rather narrow dirt road next to the river under the bridge.

I noticed a group of men watching us from the other side of the ravine. They must have been the bridge guards there, or perhaps the officers from whom our man had obtained permission for our highline by phone. I didn't see any guns, but I did see a lot of curious and astonished looks. So I decided to balance over again and perform a few tricks for the gentlemen.

They welcomed this very much, beckoned me closer, laughed, were enthusiastic about the show, and finally signaled to me with their hands and feet what I took to be an invitation to have coffee. So I balanced to the end of the line and over the manure left over from the old goat shed, luckily not barefoot.

I was greeted with applause by five rustic men. They were all dressed in the style of the first bridge keeper: somewhat military and yet comfortable. No one spoke even a hint of English. Some of them knew a few individual words in German, but at most something useless at that moment, like *Auto, Guten Tag,* or *BMW.* With my touch of Russian and their gestures with hands and feet, I understood that I should come into their room for a little snack.

The house where the bridge keepers stayed resembled an old barracks, certainly also built in the Soviet era. The decor seemed like it was from another era. The furniture was rustic and covered in dust. Faded black-and-white photos of soldiers hung on the walls. There were also a few old rifles, none of which looked like they would ever fire a shot again. The most modern device I could spot was a rotary telephone.

I followed the men into a kind of office belonging to their boss, where they immediately gave me a pile of bread and cheese and, unfortunately, the most disgusting lemonade I had ever tasted to drink. Green plastic bottles whose contents were also green! Sticky, sugary stuff full of artificial flavors. I only managed a few sips. The cheese was good, but very salty. It had to be that way. Now I was thirsty, but I couldn't quench it. They also offered me schnapps, which I politely but vehemently declined. *"Ya nje pio alkagol"* ("I don't drink alcohol")—was one of the Russian phrases I had memorized before the trip and used most often.

The chief officer tried to talk to me, speaking his deep, rough Russian very slowly but extra loudly. I only understood a few words, so I kept nodding and smiling. The content was not so important in this intercultural exchange. It was surreal. How did I end up in the office of this whatever-his-rank-or-profession Armenian? Shouldn't I be afraid? After all, I didn't know the people at all. And they had weapons. But I felt no fear whatsoever. You don't always have to speak the same language to trust each other. They had seen me highlining and now I was their guest. Men my father's age were talking to me, all of them clearly excited that a young man from Germany was sitting in front of them. I heard a few snippets about cars, some relatives or friends in Germany, and, of course, football. Hardly anyone knows less about football than I do, but whenever German footballers are mentioned abroad, I always nod with a profound look—like an expert.

When, after numerous facial and gestural requests to eat more, I finally couldn't fit anything else in, the highlight of the day came. The gentlemen took me outside and proudly presented me with their vintage car collection. Several ancient cars and minibuses, one even a VW, most of them no longer identifiable. Half disassembled, partially rusty, but clearly not yet unfit to drive. In a garage stood the classic Soviet car, a Lada, certainly a good thirty to forty years old but apparently still in reasonable condition. I gestured to ask if I could sit in the car and take some selfies with my GoPro, and they seriously pressed a key into my hand, nodded encouragingly, and made steering wheel and accelerator gestures. They wanted me to take their jalopy for a spin!

Once you've started to let go of the proverbial rudder and embrace whatever the day brings you, you don't just suddenly stop. So I took the keys, got behind the wheel, and started the old Lada, which started with a loud roar on the first try. That was worth a round of applause and laughter from the men. I think a few of them also passed the bottle of liquor around among themselves. Luckily, the vehicle was parked in such a way that I only had to roll forward.

I drove out of the garage and slowly across the yard, struggling to engage the heavy, sticky clutch. The accelerator pedal also seemed almost rusted, the engine was loud, and of course there was no power steering. The men trotted after me, laughing. I knew that the more enthusiasm I showed them, the happier they would be and the more hospitality they would add to the mix. I stepped on the gas and shifted into second gear, started driving away from them, waving out the window and shouting, "Bye-bye."

They got the joke, especially since I had previously given one of them my GoPro to film me driving the vintage car. The trust was mutual. I drove around their building once and stopped in the middle of the yard in front of the laughing, thigh-slapping men. Now they had a wonderful story for their children and grandchildren or bar buddies, which they would no doubt embellish further: "That time that crazy German tightrope walker suddenly came balancing over the ravine next to their bridge and almost crashed their ancient car. . . ."

As a farewell, they handed me a plastic bag full of bread, cheese, and one of those disgusting sodas. They gestured toward the other side of the highline and said *"tvoi druzya,"* Russian for "your friends." So I was supposed to balance back over the highline with provisions for my friends. Well, they had a lot of faith in me!

I thanked him from the bottom of my heart, attached the bag to my climbing harness, hoped it wouldn't tear or swing too much, tied myself into the safety harness, and slid out onto the highline. With every step I took across the ravine, the voices and laughter of the old Armenians behind me grew quieter and quieter.

Back on the other side, the laughter was no less hearty as I told my friends Sasha, Vova, Aidan, and Jaan about my experiences, handed them the lunch bag. Then I watched as they too fought to swallow a sip of the yellow-green sugary concoction.

Before we packed up and left, our bridge keeper had Sasha and me each pose for a photo with his rifle on our arms. What funny guys.

Power Tower Highline

"Dude, there are two towers without cables on them!" Vova suddenly blurted out.

I woke up from my half-sleep, sitting in the back of Sasha's bed, while our bus chugged along some country road through the middle of Armenian nowhere. The last thing I was consciously aware of during the journey was that we had to drive at walking pace at times because huge flocks of sheep were crossing the road in front of us. But now there was something we should take a closer look at.

In such a sparsely populated country, all power lines usually run above ground on large power poles. And what Vova discovered made us all stop and think. Two large, lonely masts stood in an open field, on which we could not find any cables even after looking for a while! A feast for highliners! We had to take a closer look at this immediately.

We zoomed around the map until we figured out which dirt roads would take us closest to the towers. With Sasha's capable Toyota, it was no problem to take paths that were otherwise only used by tractors or livestock. We walked the last hundred meters across green meadow hills, surrounded by fields, natural hedges, fragrant spring flowers, and nettles. Our view from a distance had not deceived us. There were no cables on these two power poles! They looked completely new, in light gray, with no rust on the steel and hardly any plant growth around the concrete bases at their feet. Apparently, they hadn't been standing there in the middle of nowhere for very long and were still waiting for their power cables. How lucky that we were driving along this country road in exactly this, who knows how short, time window. The plan was made without us having to talk about it much.

"Let's do it, guys!" said Sasha.

Using the laser rangefinder, we found that the towers were just under 230 feet / 70 meters high, 1,050 feet / 320 meters apart, and their tops were almost at the same height. In between there were only grassy hills and a few bushes.

While Aidan and Vova began laying out the line in the field, Sasha and I discussed who would climb which tower and what anchoring equipment we should take with us.

There was an argument, which unfortunately had been happening a lot lately. Ever since Sasha successfully completed the half-a-mile line in Kislovodsk and thus held the Russian slackline record, something had changed in him. At least that's how I felt. His ego sometimes seemed to have grown beyond reality. He was constantly bossing others around.

"Just take one fucking sling and shackle and do it like this! Why so complicated way like you?"

He seriously wanted to tell me how to set up the highline anchor and tried to convince me that my version was stupid. But maybe I wasn't much more sociable than he was. Maybe I sometimes unconsciously let it show that I had many years more experience than most slackliners.

The others mostly complied with his instructions or avoided any potential conflict. However, I definitely didn't make a secret of it when I disagreed with someone or was really annoyed by them. All the better that when we were setting up the line, we were each on our own power pole, like on our own throne, the sole rulers of our highline tower. There was a straight-line distance of 1,050 feet / 320 meters between our kingdoms. We didn't have any walkie-talkies. That was probably exactly the distance our minds needed right now. The communication was mainly done through Aidan and Vova, who handed out the slackline band in the middle.

Climbing the power pole was an adventure in itself, one I had often imagined as a child. Of course I had never seriously considered it, knowing that the risk of a fatal electric shock was greater and much less under my control than the risk of falling while climbing. Here I was finally able to realize these fantasies due to the lack of power lines. And so, with a tagline attached to my harness, which I would later use to pull the slackline up from the middle, I carefully climbed rung by rung, crossbar by crossbar up the airy, completely exposed tower. Every few grips or steps I stopped and took a break so that my arms wouldn't get too pumped up.

Once I reached the top of the tower, I secured myself and began setting up the highline anchor. It was child's play. Attach padding, sling, shackle, backup to the steel beam, pull up the line, hook it in, and you're done. Sasha took a little longer on the tension side because he secured himself with a climbing rope on the tower every few meters as he climbed. It made perfect sense, as he wanted to attach this rope at the top so he could rappel later. Additionally, we were able to climb up with safety equipment later for highlining. Since we only had one rope, I had to do without it at the static anchor and climb down the tower after tensioning it instead of rappelling.

The line was insane. Completely exposed in all directions. You could even see through the power poles and see infinitely far into the rural distance from almost every point on the Highline. And the line was even longer than the last one at 1,050 feet / 320 meters, so it would again set a new record in Armenia.

After Sasha and Vova had made a few attempts on the line, they came down from their tower and I climbed up. It was divine timing. The wind had died down and I was able to balance into the sunset.

The photos Aidan took of it still have a magical effect on me today. Up there between the power lines, I was so detached from everything. Equally from my physical surroundings, from the earth, and somehow from reality. I found myself on a narrow strip between two power poles in the middle of rural Armenia, free as a bird. From the center I could see Turkey's highest mountain, Mount Ararat, 16,854 feet / 5,137 meters high, located far to the east of Armenia's neighboring country. In between, endless, deserted distance. A few tiny villages and farms were in sight, but no one seemed to have spotted us. I enjoyed every step and took my time. Sometimes, I walked deliberately fast, sometimes I took my steps in slow motion. Sometimes, I closed my eyes for a few seconds. Sometimes, I crossed my arms behind my back. The training on the last lines had paid off. I was floating. I can't remember ever having walked a line this long that was so easy for me.

On the way back, I did some yoga poses, standing on one leg, holding my free foot in my hand: *sarvangasana*—my favorite asana. Afterward, I stood in the middle and watched the sunset in the west. There was absolute silence. I relaxed as best I could and eventually maintained my balance with only tiny movements of my wrists. I was completely one with the line, with the place, with this moment. I was grateful.

This was the first and only power tower highline ever walked by anyone, to my knowledge. The next day, Sasha also managed to walk it from start to finish, and Vova crossed it with only one fall. He too became stronger with each route and more addicted to the feeling of balance. We all loved each other again.

During my last session, I decided to do something I hadn't done in years: a leash Swami ascent, a walk where you tie the safety rope around your stomach instead of attaching it to your harness—a precursor to a full free solo. I had also been thinking about this for a long time when planning this route. It was incredibly easy for me; the conditions were perfect, and I always knew that if I wanted to top my last free solo world record, it would have to be another paradigm shift, meaning not just a few feet longer, but groundbreaking, in new dimensions. One thousand fifty feet / three hundred twenty meters would be such a new dimension. And I felt physically ready.

But something kept me from leaving out the leash altogether. I wanted to keep the record for myself. The line wasn't high enough. If I wanted to stay true to my own standards, it had to be at least as high as it was long, which in this case was over 1,050 feet / 320 meters! Once you've set a free solo highline world record, there's no turning back. Nothing can be changed anymore. You have to be happy with the place and the performance. Here it just wasn't enough for me. I also think the argument with Sasha the day before was still too fresh in my mind. Not everything was 100 percent perfect, as I needed it to be for a free solo.

Today I regret it a little bit. When I think about free solo highline world records, which I still consider the greatest challenge, I realize that you don't get an unlimited number of opportunities to do so. Maybe I should have taken this opportunity back then. Instead, I chose the Swami variant, where the commitment is not quite as great. Actually, it's stupid. If you have a rope tied around your stomach and fall in, it causes excruciating pain, often even internal injuries, and how are you supposed to be rescued before you suffocate or bleed to death? You could just leave out the leash completely. But it's a relief to feel some kind of rope on you, even if you absolutely have to catch yourself when you fall.

Of course I was a little nervous with the Swami at first, and I went slower than with a belt, almost like a free solo. But the weather conditions remained stable, and I glided over the line in flow. Fifteen minutes later I had arrived on the other side and knew I could walk this distance without any safety equipment. I was safe enough. But I let it go.

Later I found out that no one had ever walked this distance using the leash Swami variation. The others downstairs hadn't even noticed, and I didn't tell them until a few days later.

An adventure that belonged to me alone at that moment and that was nevertheless a small, unofficial world record.

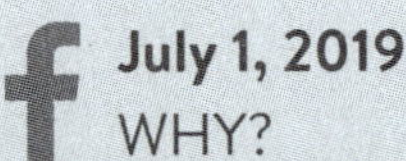

July 1, 2019
WHY?

Why go on a two-month-long road trip through the Middle East? Why travel to places far away from your home and your belongings? Why sleep outside when you could sleep in your comfortable bed? Why endure the hardship, hunger, the risks that often come with a journey off the beaten path? Why seek uncertainty when everything is easily taken care of at home? Why try to find new highlines when you could just train at home? Why free solo when you could be wearing a leash and have no consequences for failure at all? Why face your fears when you could just stay inside your comfort zone forever?

I firmly believe that it is in the adventure, in the ever-changing horizon, the unconventional and new experiences that challenge our body and our mind, that we find true and lasting happiness.
And I think if we always listened to the scared voice inside, that's telling us to stay in our nice and warm comfort zone, mankind would still be living in caves.

Iran

IRAN
END OF MAY 2019

Thanks to the permanent nature of Facebook, I still remember the words of Mahmoud, the Iranian slackliner who had invited me to his country a year earlier:

"You are the man. I mean, you are the best highliner in my mind, and I think all Iranian slacker knows you completely and really want to see you in Iran. Make us super glad if you can come for the next one. It's great for Iranian highliners to see your training and highlining here. It can improve slacklining in Iran! So you are my special guest every time that you can come. It's the pleasure of Iranian slackliners to create an opportunity for the slackliners all over the world to experience this exiting activity in Iran."

Who could say no to such an invitation?

After our adventures in Armenia, we continued our road trip south toward Mahmoud's homeland. The closer we got to Iran, the more the landscape around us changed from grassy hills and sheep pastures to desert. From green to brown to orange. The border ran along a river, with a sixteen-foot-high / five-meter-high barbed wire fence on both sides. Crossing the border itself turned out to be an odyssey. Our passports and visas were given the green light. But not our car. We needed a so-called "*Carnet de Passage*," a type of car visa that some countries use to prevent foreigners from illegally selling their cars in the country. Sasha had known about it beforehand but would have had to drive back to Moscow to apply before our trip and wait there for who knows how long. He had been sure that there must be some way to get through the border by car.

There was indeed one, but we had to wait two whole days for it. When we arrived at the border, it was Thursday afternoon and therefore the weekend in Iran. Friday is a holiday there and therefore truly holy. So we pitched our tents and broiled in the heat in the parking lot at the border. On Saturday afternoon the time had finally come and the border guard who had promised to help us finally got in touch.

In limited English, he explained how much we would have to pay for a temporary "replacement *Carnet de Passage*." To this day, I still don't really know what exactly happened. Sasha and Vova seemed to have more experience with this. They simply called it: "Corruption. There is a price for everything."

So we were given some kind of slip of paper for the equivalent of about $170, and our car was waved through. The border guard also told us that we needed another document, which he could not give us here, but that his colleagues in the next small town toward Tehran would have it ready for us. That was totally bizarre. When we stopped for the first time to buy a snack on Iranian soil, a man immediately came running up to our car, looking friendly and holding a piece of paper. He didn't speak a word of English, let alone German or Russian, but he managed to make us understand that he was a colleague of the guy at the border and that we needed this paper for our car. Crazy. We hadn't left a phone number or anything else, and we didn't even have mobile data in Iran at that point. Had he simply waited for our car on the side of the road?

Another strange moment was when we exchanged money at the border. Iran was largely excluded from the international payment system, meaning that it was not possible to pay or withdraw money there using any foreign bank or credit card. So we asked around at the border for a currency exchange office. A man stopped us before we could go to the checkout. He spoke a little English and explained that we would only be wasting our pretty $100 bills here, as the official exchange rate negotiated by government agencies was much worse than *in the streets*. At first, we didn't understand anything, suspected a scam, and could hardly believe how many rials more he wanted to give us than the official office. Was that a stack of counterfeit money the guy was trying to sell us? There were so many banknotes!

While one of us was always communicating with him in some way, the rest of us were trying to get smarter with the help of Google. It was like this: In Iran, which was economically severely sanctioned and isolated, there was massive inflation. The cash was hardly worth anything. A loaf of bread cost fifty thousand rials in the local currency. Foreign currency, especially euros and dollars, was in great demand because its value was much more stable. It was particularly interesting for black market purchases because many goods were banned in Iran and/or had to be smuggled around embargoes. These included alcohol, tech, and other Western cultural goods. By the time we finally got it, the guy was pretty annoyed by our mistrust and our lack of understanding. He had already come down a bit on his original offer but still offered us about four times as much as the official exchange. I had haggled over goods before, but never over money.

Later in Tehran we learned that we could have gotten even more for our dollars and euros there. But either way, we should live like kings for the next three weeks. Gasoline here was "basically free," as Sasha had predicted, so cheap that you hardly thought about it when filling up. And Iranian hospitality surpassed *all* the clichés one had ever heard about the Orient. After driving for almost a day in sweltering heat along dusty, littered country roads, we were welcomed by the slackliners in Tehran with more friendliness and enthusiasm than I had ever experienced on any other trip.

They almost fought over who would show us the city, invite us to dinner, and take us home. . . . To them, we were like superstars. It was a strange feeling at times, but I could understand their joy: those who don't have the freedom to travel like we Europeans do are all the happier when someone from another country comes to visit them. I was deeply moved to see these young people so open in this foreign, sometimes disreputable country. I would never have thought that before. In Tehran alone, there are probably several hundred active slackliners who meet regularly in parks to train, have founded clubs, and are all, like me, gripped by the same addiction to floating on the narrow ledge. However, only the most experienced of them were also active highliners.

In Iran, it is extremely difficult to get hold of slackline and climbing equipment or sporting goods in general. I soon discovered that there were about ten people sharing a single highlining harness. I decided early on to give away as much of my personal equipment as possible before my flight home.

I don't even know where to begin with all the wonderful, deep memories of Iran. . . . What definitely shouldn't go unmentioned, and what we were able to experience very early on in our trip, is the divine, legendary, skull-bustingly delicious Persian food.

On our first evening in Tehran, Mahmoud, the Persian slackline veteran with shaggy black hair, scattered gray strands, and a bearded, sun-tanned, perpetually smiling face, invited us to his home for dinner: His mother had already started cooking the day before when he had announced the arrival of foreign guests. In Iran, young people usually stay in their parents' home until they get married and do not necessarily move out even then. Closeness to family is part of the culture—but it may also have something to do with the horrendous rents in Tehran and the perpetual inflation. Mahmoud was unmarried and still lived with his parents in his late thirties. Although they didn't speak a word of English, they were also excited to see us. What followed was a feast. A long white cloth was spread out on the carpet in the living room, and we all sat cross-legged on the floor. There was Ghormeh Sabzi, the Iranian national dish: a truly divine stew of green vegetables and herbs, dried limes, red beans, and beef with a side dish of crispy saffron rice.

And it wasn't long before we were at our first highlines. Mahmoud told us about a spot right on the city limits in the north of Tehran, surrounded by mountains. There were already two shorter lines there that the locals sometimes set up. Before we arrived, he had already drilled the anchors for a longer, higher highline, from the center of which one could look far out over the largest city in the Middle East. We shouldn't worry about where to sleep or what to eat. Said and done.

It was truly an amazing sight. Never before had I seen how a gigantic city—Tehran had almost nine million inhabitants—ended so abruptly and a mountain range began. Of course the mountains were very different from our Alps or the Caucasus Mountains further north. More desert-like. The rocks were brown to orange-yellow and instead of meadows, forests, and grassy hills there was sand, huge gravel fields, and isolated shrubs and bushes.

Directly below our planned highline, a small river wound its way out of the mountains toward the city, with a few palm trees growing along its banks. A small oasis in the desert, just thirty minutes from the outlying residential areas of the metropolis. This is where we set up camp. There were about fifteen to twenty of us, with only slightly more guys than girls.

How? Women slacklining and highlining in Iran? Oh yes! This was something I soon discovered with astonished joy. In this country, which is so strongly influenced by Islam, there were almost as many women on the lines as men. Although guys still dominated highlining, at least the girls were already there, feeling their way around their first sky bridges and beginning to overcome their fear. One of them was nineteen-year-old Raha, who was also there now and could already walk 160-foot-long / 50-meter-long highlines. Another was Reihane, a woman in her mid-twenties, who I unfortunately didn't meet during my trip but who I had heard had even done short free solo highlines. Just imagine: There are fewer than five women worldwide who have ever walked a highline without a safety harness, and one of them is from Iran! I would soon meet another talented Iranian slackliner who changed my life forever.

But at this moment, we were still in our little oasis not far from Tehran. The midday heat beat down on us. Just the right time for a hot tea with honey and dates. We were constantly supplied by our

Iranian friends. It was their pure pleasure to sweeten every minute for us. Hospitality was truly lived here.

The heat couldn't stop us for long. We split into teams and climbed up the scree fields, holding a tagline that soon hung over the canyon and riverbed. We wanted to pull a 890-foot-long / 270-meter-long highline over it after Mahmoud wanted to hear Sasha's and my opinion on the anchor points he had established.

Somehow Sasha and I managed to argue about the setup again. Today I no longer understand how we could have slipped into that situation. A complete waste of time and energy. And somehow embarrassing in front of our new Iranian friends.

But with so much love from the locals, our spirits quickly cooled down despite 86°F in the shade, and the highline was set up. The Iranians couldn't wait to see my Russian friends and me walk across it and take photos of these international "stars" who had come to their country. . . . For them, 890 feet / 270 meters was quite a feat, but for us, it was child's play.

Sasha walked the line straight away, and Vova did the same after a few attempts. I already put my hands in my pockets on the way there. On the way back, I managed to walk almost the entire route without using my arms for balance. That would have been another new world record. A good idea for later . . .

But even among the Iranians, there was one who was able to walk the line straight away and even balance back by turning around without a break. His name was Siavash. He was twenty-six years old, a super-fit climber, and a gardener and farmer by profession. His balancing style reminded me of Julian Mittermaier: a clear sign of talent.

I enjoyed the view over Tehran, even though it wasn't that beautiful from a purely visual perspective. The huge city was simply impressive. Gray concrete and skyscrapers as far as the eye could see, punctuated by construction sites and cranes for even more skyscrapers. Below me was the desert and my friends in the small palm oasis, from which the smoke of a campfire and the aroma of grilled saffron chicken were already rising. We had truly arrived in Iran.

"No high without lows" —Alexander Schulz

Tehran is gigantic, and it takes hours to get out into nature. Therefore, most slackliners met regularly in the large urban Laleh Park to train together. I had no idea that this park would be the one that would have both the worst and the best experience of my entire trip.

First of all, we became really immersed in the Persian slackline community there. Dozens of guys and girls gathered around over ten slacklines. Rodeolines, tricklines, longlines hung crisscross, juggling balls, sticks, Frisbees, and other flow toys flew through the air. Once again, I realized how similar people all over the world are when you look beneath the surface of religion and culture. Everyone wants to live, sing, laugh, play. Even here in Iran. Maybe even especially here.

Word of our arrival quickly spread and soon we had to endure one selfie after another. The modern form of the autograph. I enjoyed it. I noticed that as soon as I entered any line, it became quiet around me and everyone was watching. Of course that gave me a boost. I surfed the lines, juggled on them, and unpacked my ancient trickline skills again. That inspired people—and I felt it.

But what was even more important to me were the conversations. Some spoke English very well, especially those who were studying, while others hardly spoke a word. But we all got along splendidly. Intoxicated by all these wonderful moments, after slacklining I forgot myself a bit in yoga and pushed myself to my limits. I wanted to see how close I could get to the lotus position. And then it happened.

I guess I hadn't warmed up enough, I was too hectic, too distracted by all the impressions around me. I pushed my knees down with my hands to force myself into the full lotus position and suddenly heard a loud, sickening crack, followed by a stabbing pain in my left knee. Shit. What had I done? I had gone too far.

I immediately tried to stretch my legs again and relax. I felt my knee swell and throb. I had seriously managed to injure myself doing yoga, and this after all the highlining, climbing, mountaineering, free soloing. . . . How could I be so stupid?

I stopped going on the slackline and just sat with the others, rested, and explained what had happened to those friends who asked me about my depressed mood.

The next day it was even worse. I was limping. The obvious thought was that everything was over now. That's it for the slackline trip through Iran. I lost all motivation. All for shit. But it didn't help. I had hurt myself countless times in my life and each time I was incredibly angry at myself and the world. I cursed the sport, felt sorry for myself, felt unfairly treated by fate. . . . But the fact is: things never got better. The only thing that helps is to make the best of the situation. To learn from it and look forward. In Iran, I didn't even have to force myself to do it, as the distraction from the bad thoughts and the support of the other slackliners were gigantic.

I took a rest day in Siavash's place, did a little work on my phone, and massaged my legs for hours to relieve pressure on my knee and improve blood flow. There was definitely nothing broken. I later learned that it was a trauma to the fibula, in which some ligaments and muscles between the fibula and the knee joint were torn and strained.

Thanks to phenomenal company, I had fun even without slacklining. Ali, an enthusiastic junior slackliner and professional physiotherapist, treated me free of charge. He said it was an honor. I was soon able to walk carefully and got myself a bandage. A day later, we did a bit of sightseeing. The day after next, I was back in the park, but I didn't do any slacklining; I just did some juggling. My friends Sasha, Vova, and Jaan, who had joined us from Estonia, were also in no hurry to get to the next highline. Everyone was in chill mode, which suited me.

We met more and more slackliners, saw different corners of Tehran and experienced one taste explosion after another in restaurants and snack bars.

Slackline Fairy Tales from One Thousand and One Nights

Meanwhile, Mahmoud, Siavash, and Mehdi organized a highline meeting in the mountainous region of Golestan, 500 miles south of Tehran. Their plan was to camp and highline there for a week with any slackliners who wanted to. We wouldn't have to worry about anything else; we would be their guests.

We drove through the night. It was tight because all the cars were full, some had slackline equipment or food on their laps, and yet I somehow managed to get a little sleep. Once again, I felt deep down that I could trust these new friends, even though I had only known them for a week. When I woke up after about eight hours of driving, we were driving more slowly along country roads, surrounded by sheep pastures and hilly forests. Again a stark contrast to the congested highways in Tehran and the desert surrounding it. At some point we parked in the middle of the forest.

"We are here, Freddy. Time to wake up," said one of the Iranians to me, visibly pleased. Somehow no one here could pronounce my name "Friedi" correctly. It automatically became "Freddy," which didn't bother me.

The drivers immediately lay down to sleep on sleeping mats right next to their cars, while the rest of us started exploring the area. Siavash led us a short distance through the forest until we came to a meadow, which after 330 feet / 100 meters abruptly broke off and ended in a vertical rock face. It was gigantic. Very similar to the South of France. Without a major mountain hike, you suddenly found yourself standing on the edge of a 660-feet-high / 200-meter-high cliff and could look down into the valley for miles. And here, too, the cliff was not perfectly straight but rather had u-shaped notches—perfect for rigging highlines.

In the evening, three lines—each between 164 and 394 feet / 50 and 120 meters long—hung high in the air, all more than 330 feet / 100 meters above the ground and providing magnificent views. During the setup, we five slackliners from abroad found ourselves in an advisory role and hardly had to help physically. The Iranians wanted to show us what they could do but still asked us for our opinion at almost every step of the construction. We enjoyed finally being able to sit back after the long journey and all the highline rigging of the last few weeks.

Of course we wanted to give back to the community as much as we could. After a few of them initially watched and then asked me if they could join in, I soon began leading extensive yoga sessions in the mornings, which eventually attracted over fifty people. And with Siavash's help as translator, I gave a "theoretical introduction to BIG Highlines" several times, talking about the physical and mental challenges of rigging and walking miles of highlines, something that many people here had probably dreamed of, but for which no one had the experience or equipment.

I saw it as my duty and somehow an honor to pass on as much of my knowledge as possible to these people. The teacher in me came through. The slackline ambassador. As in the West, so in the East.

Beginners as well as advanced slackliners appreciated my tips. The presence of international balance athletes was celebrated and made the young Persians proud of their small festival. And every day I was just grateful that I was allowed to be here. My knee was already feeling much better; I only wore the brace when walking on steep terrain, but I was already doing yoga again and walking on highlines.

As on my travels through Europe and America, one of the big highlights was the atmosphere around the campfire. The phenomenal food was now accompanied by phenomenal music. There were some exotic drums and a plucked instrument I had never seen before. It resembled a Bavarian dulcimer. And then the singing. Like the food and hospitality before, it hit me right in the heart. Farsi is an incredibly beautiful language. Honey-sweet and soft, melodic, poetic—especially if you don't understand the content. It sounds like someone is painting a picture in the air with their words. Singing around the campfire under the starry sky was a journey in itself, once again into a new land, a new world of tones and sounds. Persians, unlike Europeans or Russians, do not sing together, but usually one after the other, again women as well as men.

In fact, there were even more women singing that evening, although I can't say whether that was part of the culture or whether more women just happened to be brave enough or wanted to sing. The people of Iran are very educated, and Persian culture is one of the oldest in the world. Quite a few children grow up with regular music lessons, write poems at school, and have stories thousands of years old read to them. I felt all of this very intensely on those evenings around the campfire.

When, on the fourth evening, a DJ booth, disco balls, and some large speakers powered by diesel generators were set up in a clearing further above our campfire site, within sight of the highlines, I wasn't even surprised anymore. Young people in Iran also want to party and dance, that's clear. And in the middle of nature, far away from the suspicious glances of older generations or even the Islamic morality police, Gasht-e Ershad, one naturally does this even more exuberantly. The DJ played techno and house music, and later even my favorite music, psychedelic trance. Men and women turned the forest floor into their dance floor. In their very basic nature, people are the same all over the world. If I had been teleported here without knowing where I was, I would never have thought I was in Iran.

All around me, flickering lights from the campfire and swirling fire flow toys blended with the artificial lights of the disco spotlights. Everything was reflected by the disco ball spinning under a tree, interwoven with the shadows of the trees, branches, and leaves. It was completely intoxicating without the influence of any substances.

Everywhere, ecstatically dancing bodies were spinning and whirling around, with laughing faces, some with closed eyes, long hair. . . . Without me noticing, almost all of the women among the slackliners had taken off their hijabs, their headscarves, over the course of the evening. Some still wore it but danced no less exuberantly. Here people trusted each other. You felt free.

It was not the first and not the last time that I realized how much more I have in common with young people from faraway countries who, like me, love freedom, nature, and sport, than with many people in Germany who speak my language but often live in a completely different world. A world of stress, concrete, monotony, and fear.

"Primal is the answer to everything" —perhaps my motto

Somehow, something that was intended for me turned into a kind of gift for the Iranian slackliners. I was in top training for highlining but hadn't done any free soloing this year. The thought was often there, the old addiction, but it just never happened. I'm really particular about deciding when to take off the safety. Everything has to feel right. The line has to be worth it.

Here, I had a 250-foot-long / 75-meter-long, about 660-foot-high / 200-meter-high slackline with a wonderful view, in the middle of nature and, above all, without any strenuous climb. I was there during the setup myself, so I knew I could trust the setup. There was no wind here either.

Two hundred fifty feet / seventy-five meters is long for a free solo, longer than my first world record at Hunlen Waterfall. I hadn't walked anything that long since my second free solo world record of 360 feet /

110 meters in the South of France. Iran was our last country on this trip. In the weeks before, I had walked several miles on various highlines. Always with safety and always well within my comfort zone. Now I felt the tingling again. The line called for me. Even though it was a festival, the line was clear most of the time and potential spectators would be at least 160 feet / 50 meters away from me on the cliff. Far enough that I could hear them, but too far for them to distract me. Maybe at this distance you wouldn't even be able to tell whether I was wearing a harness or not. All in all, I rated the line and the location as suitable for solo riding.

The fact that the DJ started playing his electronic dance music at midday, about 160 feet / 50 meters from the abyss, didn't change anything. Quite the opposite. I felt like everything was coming together and an otherworldly moment was about to happen. The night before, I had seen the sunset just beyond the 250-foot / 75-meter line, and it was phenomenal. The weather was perfect.

By the early afternoon of the fifth day, I was well warmed up, I basically no longer felt the injury to my knee, and I could see clearly what lay ahead. I asked the DJ if he could do me a huge favor and play my sound right at sunset. Progressive psytrance. Powerful yet meditative. Suitable for transporting people into higher sensory states. And despite its electronic origins, it always fits in with nature: minimalist rhythms, primal, animalistic.

I made sure the DJ understood how important this was to me. I told him that my dream was to balance through the sunset to this music, but I didn't tell him that it would be free solo. I only told Sasha and Vova about the plan. They both understood me. I asked them to sit at one of the anchor points at the right time to prevent other people from getting too close to the line or touching it if necessary.

The two Russians were tough guys who wouldn't be too keen on this responsibility. They trusted me, and I trusted them, after everything we had been through together in the last two months.

As the sun approached the horizon and the trees, meadows, and rocks shimmered in the golden light of the evening sun, I did my last preparatory lap, with my harness on, in slow motion and completely in the moment. With every step I was completely relaxed, knowing exactly how the line reacted to my movements, what I had to do, and how to keep my thoughts in check. And once again I arrived at the end of the line, took off my harness and said to Sasha, Aidan, and Jaan, who were sitting at the anchor point, "This is it."

The DJ had started playing the music I had been waiting for. I slid a few feet on my butt on the belt and was completely on my own again, just as I wanted. I exhaled and did my sit start.

I took the first steps almost in slow motion. Especially at the beginning of a free solo, you really have to actively calm yourself down, get into the line, and not let the thought arise, "What if . . ." or "Get it over with as quickly as possible." But I didn't get nervous. I just functioned. The training worked. The flow was there.

I felt as light as a feather, wearing only shorts, a T-shirt, and a cap that I had pulled down quite low over my face so that all I could see was the line and the 660-foot-deep / 200-meter-deep abyss below. Complete tunnel vision. Other people no longer existed for me. The beginning and end of the line also did not exist. Just the next step and my steady breathing. I floated over the middle of the line; the other end was already close. I could hardly believe how easy it was for me. Why wasn't I nervous even at the end, at the point that is usually so difficult for me? But I breezed right through it.

As I took the last steps over the precipice and the ground was six feet / two meters below me, I noticed Vova for the first time, sitting next to the anchor point, a thick tree, grinning.

"Nice job, dude," he said and hugged me as I got off the line.

I was happy, but I still stayed in the zone. I kept one hand on the line the whole time; I wasn't finished with it yet. The timing worked out. As I sat back down on the line, shook out my arms and legs, and mentally prepared myself for the return trip, the DJ turned the music up a little louder. It was exactly my sound. Ultra powerful bass, 140 beats per minute, trance music that beams you from this earth into space. Something like that.

I waved to the DJ and gave him a thumbs-up. He couldn't have seen me the whole way through, but he certainly saw the end. He seemed excited, applauding me and dancing while tweaking the controls on his console. By now, a few people had gathered 160 feet / 50 meters away, choosing the best spots to watch me, a few meters behind the edge of the cliff. I hadn't announced anything—that doesn't work with free solo—but I had definitely consciously accepted that people would watch. The line was just so visible, and the best places around it were to sit on the grassy hills and enjoy the sunset. Well then, the Persian slackliners and the locals from the surrounding villages who had gathered here were going to get to see a sunset of the highest order.

I exhaled deeply again and stood up. This time it was even easier for me. I had a smile on my face from the first step. The situation was perfect. My dream. A borderline experience, accompanied by music, nature, and the certainty that there are friends somewhere who will support me. The sun was now just above the horizon. It wouldn't stay with us much longer. I slowed down, which isn't always easy, especially during a free solo, as you usually don't want to stay in this absurd situation any longer than necessary. Floating in the air, with no more than a one-inch-wide band beneath your feet. But anything that requires overcoming, anything that other people find absurd, appeals to me even more. I noticed the orange glow of the sun in my peripheral vision. It was now touching the horizon. The set-up was perfect: the sun was horizontal at a 45° angle to the line. It didn't blind me, but I could still see the sun while balancing. I found myself thinking how crazy the whole thing must look from the edge of the gorge. . . . The man balancing through the sunset without any safety equipment. I knew that from the right spot it would look like I was floating in the middle of the yellow fireball.

I didn't think about it for long, my attention had to continue to be focused on every step and the movements of the line. I consciously felt the band beneath my feet, consciously felt my posture, and breathed consciously. When I reached the middle of the line, the sun had already disappeared a third of the way behind the horizon, the entire sky glowed pink—the colors were absolutely spectacular. That was my moment. I stopped.

Continuing to breathe deeply and audibly, I slowly and carefully turned to the side until my feet were symmetrically turned 90° to the line. I slowly let my gaze wander from the line in front of me to the side, above the abyss, along the distant horizon. Full exposure. Now I could no longer see the line, but only the abyss below me and in front of me: endless rocks, hills and forests, all of which blurred on the gray-green horizon and finally merged into the orange-pink glowing sun. I raised my arms above my head like a sun salutation in yoga. I'm not religious, but almost anyone would describe this moment as spiritual. It was a moment of great gratitude for me.

I stood in the exposure and watched the sun set. I minimized my movements, controlled the line with only the slightest effort of my wrists and fingers, and relaxed almost all of my muscles. I slowed my breathing further with each exhale. When the fireball finally disappeared, I awoke as if from a kind of trance, the music penetrating my consciousness again. Of course I had been awake the whole time because I was holding my arms in the air, keeping my balance on the slackline, but I still hadn't noticed how time had passed. Real flow. Hard to find in modern life.

I carefully turned back toward the line and began to balance my way back. I knew I had to be careful. It was another one of those moments where you have to be aware of your ego. When everything works so well that you feel like nothing can harm you. And so I tried even harder to take every step perfectly, to anticipate every movement of the line, not to go too fast toward the end, to stay completely focused, despite the incredible experience that lay behind me.

But the experience wasn't over yet. My friends felt the same and remained completely silent the whole time. Only when I finally completed the last few steps in what felt like ultra-slow motion and stepped off the line did they burst into cheers. I hadn't noticed, but many of the Iranian slackliners had gathered at the anchor point. I let out a quick cry of joy, but the next moment I felt strange, surrounded by so many people. That wasn't the point, even though it certainly boosted the ego. And was I mistaken, or did some of the Iranian men and women even have tears of joy in their eyes? But why should I deny it or fight against it? It was an emotional affair. It was the highest feeling I knew, and somehow a little bit of it had spilled over onto the people.

I endured countless hugs, or rather, I enjoyed countless hugs. "Thank you, thank you so much, Freddy! Thank you so much for showing us true freedom, true fearlessness"—"God bless you," some also said. . . . Really crazy, I've never experienced anything like that before.

But I decided to listen to my own advice, which I had given so often to other slackliners and friends in various life situations: "Don't overthink it." What had happened had happened, and I could not have done without this visit to this place. Now it wasn't just my own experience, but something we all experienced together. In my reflections in the days and weeks that followed, and during some profound conversations with my Russian and Iranian friends, I came to the following realization: I believe that the lives of many young people in Iran are unfortunately characterized by fear. Fear of inflation, unemployment, and oppression by the regime. Fear of military interventions from abroad, fear of never being able to see the world, fear of being forgotten by the world outside. . . . Maybe it's just my imagination, but is it possible that an act of complete freedom from fear, even as banal and essentially pointless as walking a highline without a safety harness, gave them hope? Could it be that my balancing free from all fear has taken away some of their own fear?

At least I hope that's how it was.

Homa

Back in Tehran, it was time again for a big slackliner meeting in Laleh Park. And as intense as the experiences of the past week were, it was here in this big city park that I had an encounter that would change my life forever. And in a way that is so beautiful that I could never have imagined before.

After a few short slackline sessions, I was more focused on yoga that day. My muscles needed a stretch after all that highlining and the long car ride. Then I noticed a young woman who was probably part of the slackline community, but who was still doing her yoga exercises with complete concentration, a little way away from everyone else. And what exercises they were. After I took a closer look, my jaw dropped a little. The young lady performed a perfect jump-through vinyasa with ease and a smile on her face, an exercise that still seems completely impossible to me today. Her feet floated between her arms in the lotus position. She didn't tremble at all in the plank, not even in the handstand. I was fascinated.

Of course she was wearing a headscarf, but I could see that she had black-brown hair. I was so impressed by the yoga demonstration that I decided to approach her. I waited until she paused, plucked up my courage, and walked over. Her name was Homa. Later she told me that her name has a meaning, something like "Bird of Happiness" in English. All I could say was, "Right."

We did yoga together, she came to dinner with the other slackliners, and before we knew it, we had a date for the next day. And this despite the fact that before traveling to Iran I had firmly resolved not to even look at the women there and had strictly forbidden myself any romantic thoughts. That would be far too dangerous, with Muslim fathers and older brothers, with knives and Sharia law and who knows what else . . .

That's what I had thought before. But life doesn't care one bit about what plans we make. Homa and I just had to see each other again. And after four years of a sometimes-painful long-distance relationship, marked by COVID-19 travel bans, visa applications, longing, and hope, she is now my wife, and we are infinitely grateful that we both felt like doing yoga back then in Laleh Park. If anyone is curious about how this came about, I'm afraid I have to disappoint you. This story cannot possibly be told in a few sentences; perhaps one day it will even get its own book. Suffice it to say, our relationship had its ups and downs, and we had to fight harder to see each other again than I ever fought for a slackline world record. But it was worth it. We share many passions, but we also complement each other. Homa is good at meditating, I am good at exerting myself. She leads with her heart, while I tend to be more calculated. Together we maintain balance in life as well as on the human-anchored slackline that my family strung for us with their bare hands in front of the town hall where we got married. Or on the wedding highline, which Homa walked for me in her wedding dress and with a bridal bouquet in her hand. We have been through a lot together and learned a lot from each other, and we will certainly go through a lot more and learn a lot more from each other. I can barely wait for it.

But this should remain a book about slacklining and not drift into a love story, which I don't even dare to write right now. Maybe someday, together with my beloved, when we have plenty of time to spare and can reminisce in front of a fireplace about our younger years . . .

Time Jump

I am writing these lines, in May 2023, sitting in a hammock at the Wolfsschlucht, where highlining began for me. While Sasha, who now lives in Germany as a political refugee due to his work for the Russian opposition, runs back and forth along the 150-foot / 45-meter line several times, Homa crosses the 210-foot / 65-meter tight freestyle line next to it. After her session, I want to say the following to her:

"Darling, you've progressed a lot on the highline and are now ready for a very simple, game-changing truth. There is no reason to fall. You either walk, or you give up. Try to get this into your head, try to really believe it. There is nothing that will make you fall, other than your own decision to stop fighting. The line will always move and never be completely calm. So don't ever try to stop it from moving. Just go with your movements and don't fall. Don't give up. And stop being afraid of falling. It's that simple."

Farewell

It was no wonder that I spent the last ten days in Iran almost continuously with Homa. With one exception.

The mountains in Iran are high, including those immediately north of Tehran. It was absurd: all around us was desert, big city, and constant sweating, and yet on the northern outskirts of the city there was a gondola that took you to a ski resort! However, I learned from Homa that skiing at an altitude of 9,840 feet / 3,000 meters was reserved for wealthy Iranians. It's not open to everyone the way it is in Germany.

For the last highline on our trip, Mahmoud had chosen the Bandeh Ben ski and hiking area around the cute mountain village of Kemshak. But there were no gondolas where we wanted to go. Mahmoud knew that one could drive relatively high up by car and then easily reach an altitude of 11,480 feet / 3,500 meters by going cross-country and following goat paths, where he suspected there was good highline potential between the rocks. Further up towered a chain of peaks over 13,120 feet / 4,000 meters high, the name of which no one knew, not even Google Earth. Maybe it doesn't have a name at all because it's just one of many. Again, the colors, flora, and fauna reminded me of the Alps, but the dimensions were much larger. So it was exactly the right project for us.

It had been a while since we had done a highline that required real work. I was a little concerned about my knee, but with trekking poles and slow walking it was no problem. The fibula trauma healed faster than expected. So we went into real solitude for our last three days in Iran. Although that's not actually correct, we were a team of ten people, our five plus Mahmoud plus four other Iranian slackliners, including two women.

At 9,840 feet / 3,000 meters above sea level, you generally move more slowly, and you can feel the thin air. So we scrambled with extreme caution over scree fields and through steep grade 3 terrain. We soon found a campsite near a small stream where we set up our tents. We then set about exploring the area and looking for potential highline anchors. This time it was Jaan who climbed ahead with the laser in his hand and spotted the best line. Once again it was almost exactly 980 feet / 300 meters. Of course it was no coincidence that we always rigged lines of this length. We had 1,150 feet / 350 meters of webbing with us on the trip and wanted to use it as much as possible. Moreover, for many slackliners, like Vova and Mahmoud, it was a magical mark that they still wanted to break. Three hundred meters, which in many countries corresponds to one thousand feet. A good number.

By now, we were all so well-rehearsed that the setup went like clockwork, in the truest sense of the word. Mahmoud used the drill to fix one side first, then the other, while Jaan used the drone to bring the fishing line. I caught them and pulled the tagline over on the fishing line—then the actual line on the tagline with the help of Hossein, a strong Iranian slackliner who used to compete in wrestling.

This time, Jaan was granted the first ascent. It wasn't easy to walk the line. We felt the height and exhaustion of the last few weeks. The others all took a few tries. I barely managed to get through on the first try, and after that I had had enough. All I wanted to do was sit on the rock, watch my friends balance, gaze into the distance, and reflect on our experiences. The mountains were gigantic, but incredibly peaceful and quiet. In the distance, only a small section of the mountain road was visible, and the village where we had parked our cars was about 3,280 feet / 1,000 meters below us. In between there is nothing but grassy slopes, a few goats, and rocks. Above us the snow-covered peak. A worthy place to end this journey. Behind me I could already hear Vova and the two Iranian women starting to light a small campfire. That's how it should be.

On our second-to-last day in Iran, as we listened to the Persian songs around the campfire once more, ate a simple but delicious dinner, and everyone was somehow exhausted and happy, a few tears ran down my face. I knew with every cell in my body that this would not be my last trip to Iran. I just had to see these people again. First and foremost, my Homa.

THE NORTH

The Longest Slackline in the World

NORWAY
SUMMER 2018

The world's longest slackline was a logistical challenge beyond anything that had come before, long before the balancing challenge even came into play.

A few words from our "Big Highline Daddy," David Sjöström, the crazy Swede who organized the project and is also a child psychologist and father of three daughters: "As I was sitting around a campfire in southern Sweden with the Swiss highline hero Sam Volery, we had the idea of taking a giant leap in slacklining history: Instead of beating the existing record by a few hundred feet, as is usual, we wanted to go over half a mile and rig a 9,190-foot-long / 2,800-meter-long line. My job as a mediocre slackliner at best was to find the perfect spot and organize the logistics. But was it possible? How risky would it be? And where do you find this 'perfect place'? The answer is: on the Senja peninsula, high up in the Arctic Circle of Norway. Across Devil's Lake, a crystal-clear mountain lake surrounded by steep cliffs that, at least in theory, should protect it from the wind. . . . During the scouting tour, everything looked good, but on the actual project, we had more wind than expected. The weather often changed unpredictably, which made the setup very difficult, despite the helping hands of thirty slackliners from all over the world.

Luckily, we were sponsored for accommodation and meals in the fantastic Hamn i Senja, where we always met up in the evenings and gathered new strength for the next day. How such a chic hotel could tolerate a group of outdoor hippies dancing all over the property is still a mystery. As the "organizer" of the project, I was called into the manager's office several times and politely informed that we could no longer invite friends to the resort to sleep on the floor and that we could not fill our bags with food from the breakfast buffet. Not every day!"

Nine thousand one hundred ninety feet / two thousand eight hundred meters. That's about the length of an average commercial aircraft runway. Twenty-seven times as long as a football field. Seven times as long as the longest ship in the world. And at least about 6 percent of a marathon. Now imagine a one-inch-wide band that stretches across this entire distance, at a height of over 330 feet / 100 meters. How would it be to balance on this? It would be a journey.

But how do you stretch a 9,190-feet-long / 2,800-meter-long band? The lake, which is over one mile wide in the middle, was both a challenge and some help for us.

The idea was to lay out the slackline on the water using a boat and then tension it from both sides simultaneously. Since this would take several hours, we had to put Mia's crucial idea into action beforehand: using buoys to prevent the line from sinking. It was quite a funny sight: Mia and Louise from France, laden with bundles of almost fifty empty water bottles, wading through the swamp to the lake shore in their improvised rubber boots made from trash bags. It had the atmosphere of an alternative music festival. And it was by far not the only such moment. Just the multitude of languages that buzz around you every day. There were people from Germany, Austria, Switzerland, Italy, France, Spain, the Netherlands, Denmark, Sweden, Norway, Finland, Canada, Israel, Australia, Chile, and Argentina on board, and not just in the figurative sense.

Rory from Australia, Martin from Norway, and Louise from France drove across the lake in a motorboat they had borrowed from a fisherman. They laid out the line, which was marked with plastic bottle buoys every 160 feet / 50 meters, on the water, while David from Sweden, Mia from Canada, Sam from Switzerland, myself, and a few other helping hands kept the line on the shore under enough tension to allow the boat to just move forward, but not to become too slack and get tangled in the turbine. The band weighed a total of 550 pounds / 250 kilograms! Just imagine the constant multilingual walkie-talkie chatter—and the many misunderstandings. So it was no wonder that by the time we had finally laid out over one mile of webbing on the lake, it was already getting dark.

This is where we made the first big mistake of the project. We decided to anchor the over-one-mile section of the line overnight between a temporary anchor on the shore and the actual Far Anchor on the opposite 660-foot-high / 200-meter-high wall. With a good pre-tension and the buoys, the webbing should stay exactly where it was. What was one night of water contact? Surely, we would be able to continue exactly where we left off the next day. Are you kidding me?

Early the next morning, we discovered that the wind and the resulting current in the lake had moved the webbing over 1,640 feet / 500 meters to the side, despite a pre-tension of at least 3 to 4 kilonewtons! And unfortunately the lake wasn't that wide. The line had become caught in the middle, on the rocks of the shallow lakeshore, and was almost completely worn through in several places. So we had to go out on the boat, undo everything, and start over.

Luckily, thanks to the originally estimated distance of two miles, we had enough pieces of the Y2K high-tech tape with us. And the second time around, all thirty hippies were already more in sync. We replaced the damaged parts, fitted them with our plastic buoys, drove the line across, and Louise said her famous phrase in the slackline scene, "Connection is made!" with the most French accent you can imagine.

Finally, we were able to remove the damned temporary anchor on the lakeshore. The line was now completely where it belonged, and we slowly started to tension it simultaneously on both sides. At the same time, our boat crew drove along the conveyor belt and removed the plastic bottles piece by piece. The line now had enough tension to stop sinking and began to slowly lift out of the water at the edges of the lake. The moment when Rory held it down with just one hand from the boat in the middle of the lake and then let it go and soar toward the sky was magical. Loud cheers rang out from both sides of the lake, like when a football team scores a goal. We were a significant step closer to our "victory."

As David and I trotted back from the lakeshore to help the crew at the anchor above tighten the tension, we talked about how many people on our team knew they wouldn't be the ones balancing across it in the end. Nobody had any illusions. Very few of us would be physically capable of doing this, and we wouldn't have enough time to allow everyone a try. So many talented young people from all over the world had invested their time and energy, selflessly sacrificing themselves for the project, without a real chance of crossing the world's longest slackline themselves. This step, or rather these thousands of steps, were ultimately reserved only for those who had trained the hardest and thus had the best chance of setting the world record. While we were talking, one of these four chosen ones was on his way to the other side by boat to attempt a crossing to the Home Anchor. It was Sam Volery.

He, Lukas, Quirin, and I had discussed the evening before what we should take with us when crossing such a long line. It shouldn't be too difficult. Water, energy bar, walkie-talkie, and a 160-foot / 50-meter cord. Our rescue plan was: A boat would be ready below the line in case someone couldn't get through. We could then use the cord to pull up a real climbing rope to rappel into the boat.

But how realistic was that? Pulling up a rope and rappelling down under your own power when you're too exhausted to walk or even injured? If it's too windy, can a boat still be waiting below you in the middle of a large mountain lake? All questions whose answers we didn't know because no one had done it before us.

Ultimately, it was clear to us: Everyone who enters this line must do everything they can to get to the other side as quickly as possible under their own power. We called it "self-rescue."

Sam was aware of this when he made his first attempt in the early afternoon at a tension of about 7 kilonewtons (equivalent to 1,540 pounds). I couldn't see him start walking, but I knew he probably wasn't visibly nervous. The thirty-four-year-old Swiss has always been one of the happiest slackliners I have known. It was pure fun for him.

About an hour later, we heard from the boat crew over the walkie-talkie that Sam still hadn't fallen and was now close to the middle and the line needed more tension. Sam was in danger of getting close to the water. He was probably only sixteen feet / five meters above the lake. Wow. We didn't see that coming. The line was new and had probably just stretched massively. The dynamometer only showed four kilonewtons. So we put on the line grip and tightened it as quickly as we could to give Sam a chance to balance over the middle. At the same time, we proceeded as carefully as possible so as not to push him down with sudden movements.

Sam later told us that it was pretty freaky how he was just balancing above the water and suddenly, within a minute, he was lifted thirty to seventy feet / ten to twenty meters into the air. I can't remember all the details of that day. I needed a break from rigging, but a short time later I realized that Sam had fallen somewhere in the last third. He must have had to contend with some pretty strong gusts of wind. But it was tough, at least he managed to walk over 6,560 feet / 2,000 meters on his first attempt. Would I be able to do that too?

There were still a few hours of daylight left, but I was dog-tired and there was a light breeze blowing across the lake. That was no longer my day. Lukas still wanted to try, knowing full well that we might not get a better time slot. But he almost regretted it. As soon as he started walking, the wind got stronger. When he was about halfway there, it stormed and rained, and he had to turn back. I don't want to sugarcoat anything. We were all so relieved that Lukas made it off the line alive, the way it was being buffeted by the wind.

"Dude, I'm glad you're such a fast walker. You wouldn't have been able to stay on the line much longer," I said to him that evening.

"Yes, speed is everything," he replied. "It was a great experience, but it was pushed to the limit. It doesn't have to happen again."

Lukas heard "I'm glad you're alive, dude" more than a few times that evening.

August 2018

The #highline3k project here in Norway has been mind-blowing in every sense so far.
I have rarely seen such beautiful, perfect, raw landscape. To be able to just see, let alone highline in such a location is a true privilege that I am incredibly grateful for. And then today we achieved something beautiful: after a failed first attempt due to strong winds, we managed to set up the longest slackline of all time in one day. @samuelvolery, who initiated this project, was inspired by this energy and went for a first crossing. Despite 4 days of hard rigging, he made it super far!!! He only fell 600m [1,970 feet] before the end! So we know this crazy distance is possible! I can't believe this is happening. Thank you so much to this incredible team of friends who made this possible! The last few days alone have already inspired me for life.
@lukasirmler is next, and then hopefully tomorrow if the wind gods allow it, @quirinherterich and I will give this line a shot. Wish us good luck

Meanwhile, our fourth world record candidate, Quirin Herterich, and I had a difficult decision to make. The weather forecast for the next morning was perfect. Blue sky and no wind. But experience tells us that this would come at some point during the day. So which of us should get on the line first?

"I don't have a problem getting up at four in the morning, Friedi. I'm at anchor at six o'clock and start the line at first light. Then you can sleep in and have plenty of time after me until the wind comes," said Quirin.

I admitted defeat and said, "Okay, dude, go for it. I'll then wait for you at the other anchor with your shoes and supplies and walk back down the line from there. Flying change. But make sure you don't start too late."

Since then, I've often looked back on that decision and wondered what might have been if I had made the first attempt of the day in Quirin's place . . .

His crossing took a long time. Incredibly long. In total he was on the road for over three and a half hours. What incredible stamina that guy had that he could afford to walk so slowly. Was that the right strategy? He started later than planned but still had perfect conditions. Zero wind.

As Martin and I crossed the lake around 10:00 a.m., we saw Quirin roughly in the middle of the line. We drove in a wide arc so as not to distract him. Our distance and the dimensions of the line made it seem as if he were standing still.

"He doesn't want to make any mistakes," said Martin.

'He wants to send,' I thought to myself. He has the world record in mind. I wished him well, but I was starting to get a little nervous about the time. I felt fit now and couldn't wait to give the line my best. Damn it, I wanted good weather conditions, too!

When we reached the other anchor, Quirin was still about 1,310 feet / 400 meters away from us, but even from that distance we could see that he was exhausted. His arms kept rowing hard. He had been out there for over three hours now. Don't look too closely, I thought to myself, or you'll put a spell on him.

I did my warm-up exercises and mentally prepared myself for my attempt. As soon as Quirin arrived here, I wanted to take his leash and get going.

Suddenly I heard a scream in the distance and Martin said quietly: "Oh no."

Quirin had fallen. Had he given up? Had he stumbled upon a connection? Could his arms simply not take it anymore? He had the right conditions for a send. Maybe his head just wasn't ready for so much pressure. Half an hour later, after a few more falls, he arrived at our place, exhausted but still euphoric, almost high. I hugged him and patted him on the shoulder, but my thoughts were already on my attempt.

"It's just a line, Friedi. You can walk them. It's much less scary than we think. Just do it."

Okay, I thought, but I don't want to make the same mistake. I'll save enough strength for the end of the line. And pray that no wind comes.

This meant balancing quickly but with minimal effort. The first 330 feet / 100 meters were pretty shaky, but little by little I got to know the webbing better. My muscles became warmer. My thoughts calmed down. I found my even breathing, my flow. While a monotonous, driving psytrance beat sounded through the small headphones in my ears, I breathed my way forward step by step at a steady pace. When things got difficult for a moment and I was starting to feel nervous, I forced myself to smile. I was having my own self-talk again like before: "You've just started walking, enjoy it, there's no reason to fall, you can't fall, there's no giving up, etc."

At some point, somehow, without really noticing, I was past the middle, had walked one mile, had walked over one mile. For the first time, I dared to believe that I could do it without falling, that I might actually set the world record on my first attempt. I inevitably remembered crossing a 5,250-foot-long / 1,600-meter-long, very difficult line in the South of France a year earlier. Back then, despite relatively good conditions, I fell 160 feet / 50 meters before the end, narrowly missing the world record. I had been devastated. I didn't want to experience that again. No, I didn't want to think about that right now. Take every step as if it were your first, I told myself. Let the vibrations of the line glide through you, with minimal effort and zero nervousness. On and on, on and on . . .

But then something suddenly changed around me. The sky became grayer; I felt the first light gusts of wind. Less than five minutes later it started to rain and get colder. I had to walk more slowly because the sky bridge beneath me was now shaking much more than it had for the past hour and a half. The rain and wind grew stronger with every foot I covered. I was still moving forward, but my arms began to flail; I was no longer relaxed and confident.

Then came struggles that made everything I'd faced on a slackline before seem easy by comparison. Powerful waves went through the line, movements that no slackliner could have caused himself. For a few minutes that felt like an eternity, I somehow managed to throw myself back toward the middle, just before I fell, only to almost fall off the other side a split second later. Gusts of wind reaching 37 mph / 60 km/h tried again and again to tear away the tiny bit of ground beneath my feet, to destroy my last spark of hope for the slackline world record. It was as if I was fighting the weather itself. And it was already dawning on me who was stronger. I screamed at the top of my lungs, fighting for my balance as if my life depended on it . . .

But at some point, that was no longer enough.

I fell.

It only lasted a fraction of a second, but it felt like an eternity. One moment I was standing on the line, waving my arms wildly, and the next moment I was hanging on the safety rope. But in between, I somehow felt all the emotions I had ever experienced on a long line again. Every success and every failure. Each one slipping by a hair's breadth from the long-desired goal. It just seemed too familiar to me. It couldn't end like this again. Reality felt at that moment like a hard, cold, unyielding wall, and I didn't understand why it had to be in front of me.

On such long lines, you often have little reference for your movements because the entire solid environment is so far away from you, but Mia, who was relatively directly below me on the lake shore at the time, told me later that the gust of wind that finally caused me to fall had blown me and the line at least 100 feet / 30 meters to the side.

I took a short selfie video right where I was sitting now, in which you can barely hear me speak because the wind was blowing so hard, but you can guess that the water running down my face isn't just from the rain. Then I tried to finish the line as quickly as possible.

After another four or five falls and a total of two hours and ten minutes on the world's longest slackline, I had solid ground under my feet again.

This distance has never been rigged again since then. Today, I still often ask myself what would have happened if Quirin had crossed the line faster, or if I had had the best weather on my first attempt. The longest slackline in the world, maybe my world record, what if . . . ? But each time, these thoughts end with the same logical and psychologically healthiest conclusion: Why worry about something you can't change? The past is over. No longer real. Looking ahead is the only sensible thing to do.

Still, after so much effort, to miss the world record so narrowly again was devastating. I had balanced for a good 7,550 feet / 2,300 meters before the wind threw me off. I felt cheated out of the walk, felt unfairly treated by whatever higher powers were behind the weather. There was no second attempt for me or my friends because the weather became so bad that we had to abandon the entire project for safety reasons.

So a defeat. But was that really it?

Our team managed to set up the longest slackline of all time, in a breathtakingly beautiful but more than inhospitable area. I had done my best, walking fast but safely and calmly until the wind got too strong, and I even had a lot of fun doing it. The smile, I realized later, wasn't forced at all; I was genuinely happy on the line. What a unique situation, what a privilege to be able to balance on the longest slackline in the world, what a wonderful feeling to be physically capable of doing it, to no longer be afraid of it. I should be grateful for that, and I still am today. The fact that in the end the forces of nature were stronger than us humans is the most normal thing in the world. What counts is experience. And I felt how valuable this was in the following years on all my travels and in all the challenges I faced. And the real payoff came three years later in Sweden.

The Longest Seconds of My Life

LAPPORTEN, SWEDEN
2021

The dream of reaching the over-one-mile mark never left us, and in the summer of 2021, we all returned to the far north, but this time to Sweden.

The distance should be shorter this time but would still be a new world record: 6,988 feet / 2,130 meters. Admittedly, a year earlier, during our reconnaissance mission, we were rather intimidated by the breathtaking Lapporten Valley (Gateway to Lapland). The landscape there is barren and battered by wind and weather. All in all, probably one of the most unsuitable places to set up a highline. But it was precisely this challenge that drove us. Our fifteen-person team, almost all of whom had also participated in the 9,190-foot / 2,800-meter line on Senja, persisted, despite, or perhaps because of, the pandemic and lockdown, until we had agreed on a timeframe and organized a semblance of a plan and budget. When we finally met in Abisko in July 2021, also located in the Arctic Circle, our motivation and patience were finally rewarded with luck: the weather was kind to us for over a week. No wind and no rain. For a gap over 1 mile / 2 kilometres wide and 1,970 feet / 600 meters high so far north, this is almost unimaginable!

In addition, thanks to the twenty-four-hour daylight of the Arctic summer, we were able to work around the clock. Ryan Jenks from the US was there, and he and Quirin were made for each other. The two rigging nerds rushed to one side of the gorge, quickly found the right anchor, and drilled, knotted, and built as hard as they could, while the rest of the team laid out an over-one-mile-long / two-kilometer-long Dyneema® rope across the entire valley. Quirin, a graduate engineer, had built a motor-driven cable winch onto a wooden plate and drilled it into the rock. This meant that pulling the slackline over went like clockwork, apart from a few moments of shock and burned hands.

When the line was finally hanging, Quirin could hardly wait to make his first attempt. But after the long day of setup, he didn't get very far. On his second attempt the following day, he walked from start to finish, thus claiming the long-awaited world record. Finally. He really fought for it and showed it at the end with a few tears of joy, emotions that you don't often see from him. But soon he had to share the world record with his friends and fellow competitors. Lukas was next and completed the course on the first attempt. Afterward, our good friend from Dresden, Ruben Langer, managed to cross the line after having already crossed it once before and falling 330 feet / 100 meters before the end. What a machine!

And finally, it was my turn. I walked to the middle and dropped down there.

This is not a joke but a gross oversimplification of the events. I should probably go into a little more detail.

After all the years of balancing through the air, jumping off cliffs on pendulum ropes, and watching friends BASE jump, I just had to fulfill my dream of skydiving. And the discipline of BASE highlining was something completely new. There are fewer than five people in the world who have ever jumped from a high slackline with a parachute. I just had to do it, I couldn't think of anything else. But, of course, you can't just tick it off just because you're standing fairly stable on the belt. There is an incredible amount of preparation involved.

In short: I completed my skydiving training at a small airfield in Germany in the (Corona) summer of 2020 and a year later—with slightly fewer jumps from the plane than recommended—I went to a bridge in Croatia to take a BASE jumping course for beginners. This one wasn't that different from my highline courses. The learning curve is similar. The body awareness and reaction speed from slacklining helped me during the free fall from the sky and deal with the fear when jumping from the bridge. The many rope jumps also paid off, not to mention the handling of ropes, harnesses, and other life-saving equipment. Of course I made a few mistakes, but all in all, I learned quickly, not least thanks to the valuable guidance of my friends Pablo, Niklas, and Vova, who had already done thousands of BASE jumps with somersaults, wingsuits, tracking suits, and every imaginable object.

In the summer of 2021, I felt ready for a highline BASE jump. Reasonably ready. I wasn't quite sure. But I had my BASE rig with me because I knew that the opportunity to walk a 1,970-foot-high / 600-meter-high highline wouldn't come along every day. Maybe never again. Before starting the project, my plan was to simply hang from the middle of the line by my arms and let myself fall, just as I had practiced from the much lower bridge. Symmetrical and controlled. Not much could go wrong, after all I had already jumped out of airplanes at an altitude of 2,620 feet / 800 meters, with parachutes that inflated much more slowly. But as I became more and more aware of the place during the setup, with its flat, moss-covered, and completely obstacle-free valley floor and the absurd, gigantic amount of air beneath the line, the thought gradually drilled deeper and deeper into my head that I also wanted to balance on it with a parachute. Not the full distance, of course, but at least a few steps. And then just let myself fall. A direct transition from balance on the slackline to balance in free fall. *Real* BASE highlining. Even now, just thinking about it makes my heart beat faster. It is the second supreme discipline, definitely in the same league as a real free solo, but somehow also something completely different.

The fact is that this stunt exerted an irresistible fascination on me. Much more than the thought of now walking the line "normally" to hopefully join my three friends in the title of the new slackline world record, as had happened several times before. Sure, I definitely wanted that too, but it had to take a back seat for now. After all, nobody knew exactly how long the weather would last and how many times we would be able to walk the line.

On the morning of the fifth day, the line was clear, stretching straight 6,990 feet / 2,130 meters through the windless, mild summer air in front of me and practically calling me to it. My parachute was packed, and I had slept well despite a night full of daylight. Now there was no longer any doubt. I was ready for my first highline BASE jump.

Excitedly, I put on my lightweight climbing harness, then the BASE rig over it, and finally tied myself into the leash. I had David and Ryan triple-check everything. They wished me, "Have fun and stay safe, buddy," and we were ready to go.

I rolled out about 160 feet / 50 meters on the HangOver. I had put on the BASE harness as comfortably as possible, loose and rather suboptimal for jumping, but I had to balance for half a mile with normal safety first. And that's not so easy with a 17.5-pound / 8-kilogram backpack on your back. The body's center of gravity shifts, all the extraneous mass swings along with the vibrations of the line, and you can't walk nearly as fast and as energy-efficiently as you're used to.

But I had practiced in the weeks before on a 1,940-foot / 180-meter midline with a small backpack full of water bottles. This now paid off. In addition, I had no send pressure whatsoever. I just wanted to get to the middle as quickly as possible, regardless of whether I fell along the way. It still wasn't easy. I had to stand as still as possible a few times and shake out my arms. But it worked. I steadily approached the center and did not fall.

I became more and more aware of the exposed nature of the spot. It was crazy. Andy Lewis once spoke of the "orb of exposure," a concept for how exposed a highline is. What makes highlining really awesome is not just the length and height, but the total distance to any solid objects around you. The larger you can draw a completely empty sphere around the person balancing, the more intense the feeling of detachment. In this respect, the line really topped everything that had come before. A webbing a little over 0.5 inches / 17 millimeters wide between two mountains, on which a little man with a parachute on his back had now walked to the middle, sat down and removed the safety device. This line was particularly narrow at a little over 0.5 inches / 17 millimeters, which is common for ultra-long lines to further reduce susceptibility to wind.

I had thought through everything as best I could, brought my own leash, and a removable leash ring. Of course I didn't want to spoil the potential send for the people after me by making them stumble over a small aluminum ring on the line. I stuffed both into my pants and tightened the buckles on my BASE rig as much as necessary. I waved to Jojo's drone, which was hovering in the air next to me about fifty feet / fifteen meters away, ready to capture the upcoming event as best it could. I took out my phone and sent a message to the project's group chat: "I'm gonna jump in the next ten minutes. Love you guys and see you later," with a kissy smiley at the end to liven things up a bit.

Then I checked all the straps and pockets again, took one last deep, powerful breath, and stood up. The feeling was completely surreal. I could hardly believe where I was. Unsecured, 1,970 feet / 600 meters above the ground, with half a mile of webbing in front of me, half a mile of webbing behind me, and a parachute on my back. But the line was silent. I had the situation under control. I didn't tense up but breathed out slowly and took the first step. Then the next one. Incredibly slow and careful but still determined. So in the end I went further than planned, almost 160 feet / 50 meters. Just before the next connection I stopped and slowly began to turn to the side. The feeling was divine. I lived my dream. The adrenaline level was exactly where it should be. My body and mind were electrified, more alert than ever before, and yet there was no paralyzing fear, no unnecessary tension, no panic. The magical state of consciousness that no substance in the world can give you. My meditation. I let my gaze wander through the valley, a little to the right, a little to the left. Somewhere on both sides were my friends, smaller than ants, but I thought I could make out a few orange dots. Those must have been the tents. To my left the sun is halfway up in the sky. It was about 10:00 a.m. on one of the best days of my life.

I thought of my friends, my family, and my beloved Homa. About how much had happened since I first wobbled around on a small slackline at the age of nineteen. And that nothing was really impossible. I checked one last time that the pilot chute was easily accessible on my lower back under the main chute container, exhaled, and let myself fall forward. Time slowed down. No, rather, my perception and my thoughts accelerated immensely. My body was by no means moving slowly through the air. On the contrary. I got a spin from the line, flipped over, and started doing forward somersaults. I had expected this beforehand, as it is almost impossible to fall off a long slackline without somersaulting, but I had *clearly* underestimated it. I had never been spun upside down so quickly before, not even when I had intentionally done three, four, or five forward somersaults out of the plane. This had to stop.

When I was standing on the line, I had everything under control, but now I was staggering, almost losing my bearings. Where was down, where was up? How much time had passed? Probably not even three seconds, my mind was racing, but I couldn't say for sure. I had previously read extensively about acceleration in free fall and knew that 1,970 feet / 600 meters meant almost exactly fifteen seconds from takeoff to impact. Given the two to three seconds it takes for a BASE chute to fully open, I ideally wanted to be stable in the air and throw my pilot chute after seven to eight seconds; ten seconds would be the absolute limit.

What must my friends have thought as they watched the whole thing live from a distance or on Jojo's drone screen? Did time also stand still for them? By now I had rolled over three or four times and had probably somehow spun around my own longitudinal axis several times. This had to stop at some point! I pushed my stomach down even further. Maximum arch, like in the very first parachute jumps, to become stable. Finally I fell fast enough to take advantage of the air resistance. I heard the noise in my ears getting louder and felt the rotation I was in slowing down.

In the split second when I next saw ground beneath me, I grabbed my pilot chute without hesitation, found it immediately, and hurled it with full force as far away from me as I could. I rowed a little more with my arms and probably rotated a little more in the horizontal plane but managed to keep my eyes on the ground.

In those one or two seconds I knew everything was okay. I had control back. Damn, what an awesome feeling that was.

The parachute opened abruptly, my legs were flung around, and suddenly I was hanging there, and the free fall was over. A hard opening, but now I was gliding slowly through the air, with a beautiful, bright yellow canopy filled with air above me. I had a 270° line twist, but I quickly released it, grabbed the control lines, and then I turned and flew toward a particularly flat-looking area of the vast, rock-dotted grassland below me. I didn't even try to stick the landing; after all, I was only wearing my super-thin slackline shoes and didn't want to injure my feet on an invisible rock at the last moment. Especially not now, when I had a four-hour hike ahead of me in these very thin shoes. So I rolled off and took the opportunity to lie down on the grass.

Wow. I had done it. So this is what a BASE highline walk and jump felt like. I looked up at the sky and just had to laugh. I later saw from the video footage that I had only been in free fall for seven to eight seconds, and the parachute flight had lasted almost forty seconds. So in what seemed like an eternity, I hadn't even fallen half the total height. It's crazy, this distorted perception of time in different situations. Did Einstein also think of such stunts when he wrote down his theory of relativity?

Suddenly, Jojo's drone was less than thirty feet / ten meters away from me. My friends basically flew after me to see if everything was okay. That was clever because there was no cell phone reception down here. I sat up and waved toward the small unmanned aerial vehicle, laughed again, and shrugged. The next moment, the drone briefly rose three feet / one meter higher and then descended again three times in a row. Funny. This was probably a kind of nod, wave, or thumbs up.

It was just a small, cleverly constructed pile of plastic, batteries, and computer chips floating in the air, but in that moment, it gave me a warm, cozy feeling of not being alone. After he flew away again, I lay there for a while until my heart rate calmed down and I had somewhat processed what had just happened. And then I started the long climb with a big grin on my face.

Words by Quirin

"Secretly, I was a little jealous of the new possibilities that the parachute offered Friedi. When he finally jumped off the slackline, it looked to us like he was falling forever. For a brief moment I thought I was going to see my friend die. In the end, this was mainly due to perspective, and the jump went more or less as planned. In any case, we never get bored."

* * *

In the early afternoon, I arrived at the western Lapporten mountain, just in time to watch David complete the last few feet of his crossing. Our "Big Highline Daddy" had finally managed to cross a world record line. He had taken off soon after my jump, fallen into the leash about fifteen to twenty times in total, rested for a long time each time, and even had a small backpack with a hydration pack on his back. We hugged and congratulated each other on the "crazy shit you just did." Then we sat on the rock with Ryan and Lukas for hours, laughing, celebrating with canned ravioli, and watching the rest of the team during their sessions while the sun just wouldn't set above us. And the next day I ran walked the line as well.

I don't want to say it was easy. But it wasn't too difficult either. I had already gotten to know the line before and had done some training by walking to the middle with a parachute on my back. And I was both euphoric and relieved after my baseline jump. I had achieved my biggest goal and put hardly any pressure on myself during the walk. I wanted to do it, I wanted to be one of the four to walk the first world record over 1.25 miles / 2 kilometers, but I knew that even if I failed, I still wouldn't go home sad.

The conditions were still perfect. Bright sunshine, hardly any wind, and ideal line tension. As always, I balanced slowly at the beginning, faster in the middle, and slower again toward the end. I noticed how years of training on long lines and dealing with pressure had made me adept. All I had to do was concentrate on my breathing and posture and relentlessly take one step after another, each one as if it were the first. Just don't think too much, just balance. That was the whole secret. Of course there were also shaky moments. I had to struggle a bit a few times. I was nervous about the leash ring getting caught when walking over the connections, I was sweating, and my shoulders were burning. But my mind remained calm the whole time. I thought of Homa several times during my visit. I saw her face before my eyes in the form of a smiling sun, telling me over and over again: "You can do this. I know you can do it. I'm proud of you." This mantra from the mouth of my beloved literally carried me over the line.

As the last seventy feet / twenty meters became steeper and I walked more and more slowly and cautiously, I felt the pressure of the finish line, but I didn't let it deter me. I even wish the line had been longer! I felt like I could keep walking forever.

During the last steps, I noticed the anchor point and the camp on this side for the first time, as we had already split into two groups on the approach, one per mountain. It was a flat rocky plateau on the summit of the eastern Lapporten mountain, where friends I hadn't seen in the last few days were now waiting for me. Among them was Quirin, who had swapped his shoes and sleeping bag with David after the two had crossed the line in different directions.

Always funny, the Big Highline logistics. I was already over the edge, but I wanted to balance the last few steps about three feet / one meter above the rock to the A-frame where the line ended. When I finally sat down, I was able to touch the weblock with my outstretched hand. It couldn't have been cleaner. I crossed the line in one hour and twenty-one minutes, making me the second fastest after Lukas. And most importantly, I was confident the whole time that I would succeed, free from doubt and fear.

When Quirin, Martin, and the others hugged me a moment later, I felt complete.

Four sky-stormers, four friends, had finally cracked the 1.25-mile/ 2-kilometer mark in slacklining. With our combined efforts, our team brought home the long-awaited world record and got revenge for the failed line in Norway. My long-standing dream of a BASE highline walk had come true, and emotionally for me it was definitely in the same league as my greatest free solos. And all of this not on just any line. Lapporten is still my third favorite among the most beautiful highlines I have ever walked—alongside Eichorn Pinnacle and Moscow City.

A good time to retire and end your slacklining career?

Let's see.

My Center

How time flies—that's what I sometimes think when I watch Homa or my sister Lulu, who is now also addicted to slacklining, as they struggle across 330-foot-long / 100-meter-long highlines. It fills me with pride and is at least as much fun as crossing my first gorges. Or when I'm presenting at competitions, like just now, three days before I write these lines, at the Red Bull Slack Warrior in Estonia. Incredibly talented and equally lovable young people from all over the world race from the line to unimaginable heights, twisting and turning as if there were no gravity. When did I try my first tricks on the narrow tread—wasn't it just yesterday?

On occasions like these, I also feel how much potential there is in slacklife, what is still possible, worldwide. Our dreams are far from over, neither on the ground-level trickline nor on the aerial highline. There are still many countries that want to be slacked, there are plenty of peaks that want to be connected, gray cities that could be decorated with our lines.

My compass hasn't even pointed in every direction yet; there are still a few abysses on this planet that are calling out to me. My friends and I just can't sit still.

The team from Norway and Sweden is currently planning an even longer, even higher, and definitely BASE-highline-suitable line, again in a completely surreal location. And my dream of a real sky highline, namely between two hot air balloons, is also beginning to take shape on the horizon. So my adventurous life will continue, different than before, but still true to the motto: make the most of every day, get everything out of the moment, all that is within it in terms of joy, happiness, and fulfillment. Pain, stress, despair, defeats, exhaustion—all of this only serves to make us feel the beauty more deeply, and it also fades with time. Good this way.

This book is, last but not least, my attempt to pay tribute to the slackline world and express my gratitude for the adventures, the unforgettable moments, and the life lessons. The stories I have told here are just a small selection, and they certainly weren't easy for me to tell. So much has happened that a book alone is not enough to cover. Unmentioned journeys, even world records.

In September 2018, I set a slackline world record of just over 6,230 feet / 1,900 meters in Quebec, Canada. I have omitted many "smaller" records, such as the urban highline world record over Munich's Olympic Stadium in 2016. In fairness, I should also mention that our world record of almost 6,890 feet / 2,100 meters was broken in France last summer and now stands at almost 8,860 feet / 2,700 meters. This time I wasn't there, but Mia Noblet and seven other young sky-stormers were.

A sign that the sport is still evolving massively. And even my second free solo world record, which I set with a length of just under 362 feet / 110 meters and a height of around 820 feet / 250 meters in autumn 2017, shortly after finishing my studies in the South of France, didn't make it in here. And this despite the fact that, as the world's first free solo ascent above the 330-foot / 100-meter mark, it was perhaps my greatest achievement in slacklining ever—and undoubtedly the fulfillment of a personal dream.

But somehow it didn't happen while I was writing, and I didn't want anything to repeat itself in this book. Instead, I realized and accepted that I keep drifting away from the sport of slacklining itself and toward thoughts and feelings that are bigger than this narrow band that I love so much. Above all, the realization that all of us who are part of this wonderful, crazy world have the same desires, dreams, and fears, regardless of our nationality, culture, or skin color. That physical and mental limits can be overcome if we don't allow our fear to hold us back. Freedom and balance may be states that can never be achieved 100 percent. But in constantly striving for it, I have found fulfillment. And maybe you will too.

Thanks

I would like to thank everyone who helped me with the book, especially Edda, Nils, and Didi, as well as the many brilliant photographers, especially Vale, Aidan, and Johannes.

I thank my friends for the unforgettable adventures. You know who you are.

I would like to thank the slackline community worldwide for all the inspiration, openness, and hospitality.

Last but not least, I thank my parents, my family, and my sweetheart Homa from the bottom of my heart for your love and understanding.

Glossary

A-frame A-shaped frame with which the ►slackline can be redirected or raised to a desired height; usually made of wood

Back bounce Trick where you fall onto your back on a ►slackline and bounce back up

Backup Backup line for ►highlines; usually a second slackline band or rope that is anchored separately from the ►mainline and glued or sewn to the mainline every few feet

Barrel roll ►Bounce trick where you grab the line with your hands and rotate around it once without your feet leaving the webbing; looks like a crooked ►Yoda roll

BASE, BASE jump Skydiving from fixed objects; BASE stands for Building, Antenna, Span, Earth; the four categories for jumpable objects

Bolt Bolt hook

Bouncing Jumping up and down a ►slackline

Bowline/Bulin Safety knot for climbing and highlining; alternative to the ►figure-eight knot; easier to undo

Butt bounce Trick where you fall on your butt on a ►slackline and bounce back up

Catching Recovering yourself on the ►slackline to avoid falling into the ►leash, often with hands and legs; the last resort in a ►free solo

Chongo mount A technique to stand up, especially popular with highliners because one leg hanging off the line provides more control; alternative to the sit start, named after "Chongo Chuck," a legendary American slackliner and vagrant who lived in Yosemite Park for a long time

Connection Link between individual segments of a long ►highline; here, the ►backup is usually connected to the ►mainline in order to have a lower fall height in the event of a mainline failure

Crossing Walking a ►slackline/highline from one side to the other, possibly with falls or breaks; a crossing without falling becomes a ►send.

Double fisherman Grapevine bend; knot used to join two ropes together

Dumpster diving Stealing food from supermarket trash cans

Dynamic tricks Slackline tricks with a lot of movement, e.g., ►butt bounce, ►Yoda roll

Dynamo Load cell; indicates how much load is on a tensioned system

Dyneema® Ultralight, very tear-resistant synthetic fiber; Dyneema® slackline webbing is mostly used for very long distances due to its low weight and high breaking load, but it is more slippery and has sharper edges than regular ►polyester or ►nylon slackline webbing

Exposure Subjection; vulnerability

Exposure turn Turning sideways on a ►slackline, usually a ►highline, and enjoying the full exposure, or forcing yourself to look into the abyss, into nothingness; a big challenge, especially for highline beginners

Figure-eight knot Standard safety knot for climbing and highlining; has the shape of a figure eight

First ascent Walking a slackline for the first time

Free solo Highlining or climbing without safety equipment.

Full man Walking a ►slackline or ►highline in both directions

Grigri Belay or backup device from the sport climbing sector

Half man Walking a ►slackline or ►highline in only one direction

Half rope Very light climbing rope, which is normally only used in double strands

Handheld ►BASE jumping technique for lower jumps, where you hold the ►pilot chute in your hand during takeoff and throw it into the relative wind after a few seconds in order to quickly open the ►main chute

HangOver Carabiner with a 1-inch-wide / 2.5-centimeter-wide ►pulley for sliding over the ►highline; using a HangOver is the alternative to crossing a highline when balancing doesn't work

Highline ►Slackline that is so high that a fall would result in serious injury or even death; as a rule, a highline is defined as one that is about thirty feet / ten meters high

High-tech webbing Ultralight slackline rope with low stretch and high breaking load; usually ►Dyneema® or Vectran®; mainly used for particularly long ►slacklines

Hourglass Hourglass-shaped handle on the rock or hole through which you can thread a loop or rope; natural way to secure yourself when climbing without bolts

Landing point A platform at the end of a climbing route or between two lines; usually secured with several bolts

Leash Safety device while highlining; usually a piece of rope (climbing rope or similarly strong rope) three to six feet / one to two meters long; it is connected with a ►figure-eight knot or bowline to the ►leash ring on one side and to the belt of the highliner on the other side

Leash ring Safety ring for highlining; steel or aluminum ring with a diameter of approximately two inches; usually, two of them are used, which are glued together with adhesive tape; before tensioning a ►highline, the ►mainline and the ►backup are threaded through these rings; when balancing, the ►leash always slides along with the slackliner

Line twist Twisting of the lines that connect the ►main chute to a skydiver's harness

Longline Long ►slackline relatively close to the ground, usually from about one hundred feet / thirty meters in length but has never been precisely defined.

Loose Relaxed; not very tight

Main chute Parafoil that slows the fall during skydiving or ►BASE jumping; is pulled out of the container on the jumper's back by the much smaller ►pilot chute and fills with air

Mainline Main ►slackline in highlining; the line that is stretched and on which one balances

Midline ►Slackline that is usually high enough to be walked with a safety harness but may not deserve to be called a ►highline. This often includes slacklines that are sixteen to thirty feet / five to ten meters high or those that are only slightly exposed and do not "feel like a highline."

Multi-pitch Climbing tour using multiple lines; a climbing route that is so long that it cannot be climbed on one line but requires breaks at several so-called belay stations

Munter hitch Half-mast throw; rappel knot that allows you to rappel or lower taut ropes using only a single carabiner

No-fall zone Area at the beginning and end of a ►highline where the ►leash fall can lead to a collision with the wall or objects below, often because highlines are lower at the edges than in the middle; this is usually omitted when walking a highline in order to avoid taking too great a risk

Nylon Synthetic fiber for ►slacklines with particularly high stretch; as a rule, shorter ►highlines and so-called freestyle highlines are made with nylon bands

Off-level When one anchor is higher than the other on a ►highline, and the slackliner, therefore, has to balance uphill or downhill

Onsight Walking a ►slackline or climbing route on the first attempt

Padding Protective material for ►slacklines, ropes, or anchor slings against abrasion and sharp edges

PCA Pilot chute assist; ►BASE jumping technique in which someone stands behind the jumper holding his ►pilot chute and pilot chute connecting line in his hand so that the ►main chute is pulled out of the container immediately after jumping; usually used for particularly low BASE jumps and for beginners

Personal anchor Short piece of rope or sling used by a climber or ►rigger to secure themselves

Pilot chute Small parachute thrown into the relative wind by the parachutist in order to pull the ►main chute, which is connected to it by a line, out of the container

Pitch The length of the line; part of a multi-pitch climbing route

Polyamide Nylon

Polyester Synthetic fiber from which most slackline straps are made; typically used for beginner ►slacklines, ►longlines, ►waterlines, ►rodeolines, and slightly longer ►highlines;

however, due to its high weight, it is rarely used on very long or world record slacklines (½ mile and more).

Pulleys Rollers; often an abbreviation for ►pulley system

Pulley system Roller pulley or cable pulley for tensioning ►slacklines

Removable bolt Drilling hook with twist lock that can be pulled out of the wall after use

Rig Can be used in a variety of ways, e.g., for the entire setup of a ►slackline or ►highline, that is ►mainline and ►backup, as well as all anchoring material together; in skydiving, the rig includes the harness, the container, and the parachutes, that is everything the jumper has on his body

Rigger Someone who builds something or sets something up

Rigging To set up something, usually using ropes, straps, fasteners, and the clever use of mechanical laws; we use it for setting up ►slacklines, especially ►highlines, but also ►rope jumps; but it is also used by parachute attendants and event technicians

Rodeoline Particularly loose ►slackline that hangs in a U-shape between two anchors without any tension; it is usually particularly difficult to stand on but excellent for swinging from side to side, see ►surfing

Rope jump Pendulum jump into a long, dynamic rope, usually a climbing rope, which is attached to a bridge, ►highline, or rope bridge; the slightly more interesting alternative to bungee jumping

Rope swing Often used synonymously with ►rope jump, with the emphasis here being on the swinging; a rope swing does not necessarily have to involve a free fall; basically nothing more than a big swing

Sack stitch Knot used for climbing; is mostly used for attaching bands and slings to anchor points; on the rope, it is a poorer alternative to the ►figure-eight knot and is used more for securing material than people

Sag Slack; loss of height in the middle of a long ►slackline or ►highline due to its stretch

Scrambling Overcoming rough terrain; somewhere between climbing and walking

Send To complete a ►slackline from start to finish (apart from the ►no-fall zone) without falling or to finish a climbing route; usually, the goal of a ►highline crossing; particularly interesting for slackliners when a new highline is used for the first time: "Can he/she make the send?"—"Did you send the line?" Even a world record only counts if it was a send

Setup Used synonymously with ►rig but with emphasis on the slackline straps; the ►mainline and the ►backup of a ►highline together make up the setup; particularly interesting for slackliners, as some setups are easier to walk than others (lightness, stretch, etc.)

Shackle U-shaped bracket that can be closed with a screw or plug bolt to connect two parts; usually made of steel; in slacklining, standard for attaching the ends of the ►slackline with the anchor points

Side-sag When a long ►slackline or ►highline bends, due to strong crosswinds, to the side in the middle instead of downward as usual; an indicator of particularly strong wind is, for example, if, despite the slackliner's own weight, it is in the middle of the line, not only below the direct line between the anchor points but also next to it; when I crossed the 9,190-foot-long / 2,800-meter-long highline, I had a side-sag of over 160 feet /

50 meters just before my ►leash fall, meaning the wind pushed me 160 feet / 50 meters to the side from the natural line

Slab Inclined slab or rock face encountered when climbing

Slacklife Lifestyle and mindset of a thoroughbred slackliner; term coined by Mr. Slackline himself, Sketchy Andy Lewis, and stands for everything we love about slacklining: freedom, adrenaline rush, nature, community, parties, adventure, living in the moment

Slackline Loose band on which you balance—the common thread that runs through my life

Sloper Inclined grip used for climbing that often requires a lot of strength or friction

Soft shackle ►Shackle made of ►Dyneema®, a soft loop of rope that tightens under load

Static side Side of a ►highline on which there is no tension, on which the ►slackline is only attached, and where you, therefore, have to do less ►rigging

Static tricks Static slackline tricks in which you statically assume certain positions or perform certain moves, e.g., double knee drop, ►exposure turn, and various yoga poses; in contrast, there are dynamic tricks, such as ►butt bounce, ►Yoda-Roll, etc.

Surfing Swinging a ►slackline from side to side—my favorite highline trick

Swami Type of safety device used in highlining where, instead of a climbing harness, you tie a thin band, a loop, or the ►leash itself around your stomach, so that a fall would not result in death but would cause great pain or even injury. A kind of precursor to the ►free solo, but you should definitely not fall during it

Tagline Cord or rope (usually thinner and lighter than a normal climbing or static rope) with which you pull the ►slackline across a ravine or from one anchor to another

Tandem slacklining Two or more climbers hanging on a common rope in a route

Tape To connect the ►mainline and ►backup every few feet with tape to ensure the setup swings evenly, prevent tripping over the backup, and allow the ►leash ring to slide along smoothly

Tension The state a line achieves by being stretched to a certain degree of tightness from one end to the other, to pull the slackline tight

Tensioning side Side of a ►highline on which ►tension is applied, usually with ►weblock and/or pulley, and on which there is, therefore, more ►rigging to be done

Tight Opposite of ►loose, tightly stretched

Trickline ►Slackline, usually two inches / five centimeters wide, twice as wide as a ►highline or ►longline, which is stretched so tightly that you can do acrobatic tricks and jumps on it like on a trampoline

Waterline ►Slackline over water

Webbing Slackline strap

Weblock Band clamp to which the slackline band is attached or clamps itself; can also be used for tensioning

Whipper Fall into the ►leash

Yoda roll ►Bounce trick in which you grab the line with both hands while standing in the ►exposure turn and do a forward somersault around it

About the Author

Friedi Kühne was born in Erlangen, Germany, and grew up in Rosenheim close to the Alps. After graduating high school, he obtained his teaching degree in English and Mathematics at the Ludwig Maximilian University of Munich. He graduated from university in the fall of 2017 and has lived in Bad Aibling since, dedicating most of his time and energy to slacklining. In late 2023, he published his first book about his slackline adventures.

During his childhood, Kühne enjoyed skiing, hiking, and mountaineering. As a teenager, he developed an interest in parkour, free running, gymnastics, bouldering, and rock climbing. At the age of nineteen, he stood on a slackline for the first time and—in his own words—became "addicted to this feeling of balance."

Despite his initial focus on tricklining, he proceeded to walk more and more highlines in the surrounding Alps. After a college exchange year as a language teaching assistant in the United States in 2015, he shifted his professional focus fully to highlining. Kühne achieved several world's first highline crossings over 330 feet / 100 meters long in popular areas along the Pacific Coast, including Yosemite, Squamish, Smith Rock, Leavenworth, Joshua Tree, and the Columbia River Gorge. During this time, Kühne also became friends with prominent American slackliners like Jerry Miszewski, Andy Lewis, and Spencer Seabrooke. Kühne set a total of sixteen slackline world records between 2015 and today.

Besides his part-time high-school teaching job, he makes a living doing highline shows and motivational speaking.